SLA GUIDELINES plus

Crossing the Divide

LRC Induction and Transition Strategies

Geoff Dubber

Series Editor: Geoff Dubber

Acknowledgements

Many thanks to everyone who has contributed ideas and discussion in my many Induction/Crossing the Divide INSET workshops over recent years. Special thanks to all friends who contributed case studies and as ever particular thanks to Sally Duncan for suggesting text changes and to the excellent SLA office Publications Team of Richard Leveridge and Jane Cooper for all their brilliant support, good humour, dedication and hard work. As always – any mistakes are mine.

As with the previous edition, the SLA would like to acknowledge Paignton Community and Sports College, Marie Hewitt and Anne Taylor for their story *Perfect, Peace and Quiet* although copyright ownership is not clearly identified. Every effort has been made to determine ownership of copyright without success. Any infringement is unintentional and will be acknowledged if the rightful copyright owner contacts the School Library Association.

Published by

School Library Association
Unit 2, Lotmead Business Village,
Wanborough, Swindon SN4 0UY

Tel: +44 (0)1793 791787   Fax: +44 (0)1793 791786
E-mail: info@sla.org.uk
Web: www.sla.org.uk

Registered Charity No: 313660
Charity Registered in Scotland No: SC039453

© 4th Edition, Geoff Dubber 2009. All rights reserved.
ISBN: 978-1-903446-52-2

Cover photographs by Phil Cooper
Printed by Holywell Press, Oxford

Contents

Crossing the Divide
Introduction	3
The Wider Picture of Primary–Secondary Transfer	6
New Intake Induction – Key Thoughts	8
Getting Started	11
The LRC Profile/Questionnaire	15
Curriculum and Reading Continuity	16
Impress the New Parents/Carers	19
Keep Consulting!	21
The Summer Term Induction Event	22
Planning the Autumn Term Session(s)	24
The Autumn Term	29
Remember the Other New Students	32
Transition for the 14+ Examination Course Students	33
Sorting the Sixth – the 16+ Students	35
Preparing to Move On	41
Adults Only	44
Conclusion	49

Case Studies
Case Study 1
Broke Hall Community Primary School	51

Case Study 2
East Barnet School	55

Case Study 3
Werneth School	59

Case Study 4
City of London Academy, Southwark	63

Case Study 5
Pembroke School	68

Case Study 6
Cheadle Hulme High School	73

Appendices
Appendix 1a
National Literacy Strategy Objectives	78

Appendix 1b
National Literacy Strategy Objectives (Answers)	79

Appendix 2a
Making Links with your usual partner primary schools	80

Contents

Appendix 2b
Check List for visiting a partner primary school   81

Appendix 3
LRC Profile   82

Appendix 4
Top 20 Induction Activities   83

Appendix 5
Induction Certificate   84

Appendix 6
Sixth Form LRC Contract   85

Appendix 7
LRC Induction for adults new to the school   86

Supplement – Short Story
The Adventures of Wordsworth the Library Owl:
'Perfect Peace and Quiet'   87

Guidance for Welsh schools –

The best transition policies have well developed arrangements, between primary and secondary schools for

- Joint curriculum planning so that schemes of work build on what has been taught previously
- Pastoral links for meeting pupils' personal and social needs
- Continuity in teaching and learning methods
- Developing pupils' literacy, numeracy and ICT skills and
- Evaluating the impact of the policy and improvement initiatives on standards.

— Extract from *Moving On... Effective Transition from Key Stage 2 to Key Stage 3*, p.5. January 2004

Please note:
For the purposes of this publication the terms school library and LRC – learning/library resource centre – are interchangeable.

Introduction

As summer holidays draw to a close so thoughts turn to the start of the new school year and the changes that it will bring. The opening weeks of the new school year are exciting, challenging and hectic. There is an influx of new students and staff to meet and greet, other students are moving up a year and established staff are accommodating new patterns of work and relationships.

It's a time for meeting new colleagues, class mates, responsibilities and workloads and coming to terms with new timetables, routines and procedures. We can all find changes hard to cope with and this may contribute to the dip in academic performance for many pupils in Key Stage 3. The motivation problems and lack of focus experienced by many lower secondary age students and the difficulties that 14+ and 16+ students often have in adjusting to the demands of new courses are challenges that the Government has focused on.

> *In Year 7 a small minority of pupils dipped by a National Curriculum Level or more in English (5%), ... Year 8 showed a substantially increased proportion of pupils dipping in English (21%)... Pupils are more likely to dip in Year 7 or Year 8 if they are Black or Asian, have special educational needs, or have a lower socio-economic status.*[1]

> *Anecdotal and research evidence suggests that there is a dip in pupil attainment at the point of transition from primary to secondary schooling.*[2]

Clear and supportive induction and transition arrangements are crucial to the well being of all students in every secondary school. Effective transition programmes and induction with an emphasis on continuity can help to develop self confidence and positive attitudes in the newcomers and contribute to a focused working environment for everyone else. Given that the school library resource centre (LRC) has a central role to play in the life and learning of the school and in establishing and developing curriculum continuity, then LRC staff have a key role to play in the induction and transition processes across all school years. In fact it is such an important issue and covers the whole range of students from Year 6 to Year 13 that it would be useful, given generous staffing levels, to allocate an entire library post in a large school library solely to induction/transition responsibilities and activities!

Indeed the need for effective and seamless induction and transition across the school has been highlighted in a number of government documents over the last decade, including *Improve Your Library: A Self Evaluation Process for Secondary School Libraries and Resource Centres*.

---

[1] Pepper, David. *The Key Stage 3 Dip: Myth or Reality*. Briefing Paper on the dissertation for Master Research at King's College London, August 2007.
[2] Spotlight 89, University of Glasgow. *Negotiating the Transition to Secondary School*. Graham, C., Hill. M. September 2003.

Is there a structured LRC induction programme which is built on as pupils move through the school?[3]

How effective are induction arrangements for pupils?

A smooth transition from the primary to the secondary stage is crucial to ensure continuity and progression in pupils' learning.[4]

Schools must ask themselves why it is that many pupils who perform well in P7 mark time or even regress in S1 and S2.[5]

The transition from Key Stage 4 to post-compulsory education can bring difficulties for students. These include settling into different work patterns with timetables that give them more control over their time; facing different levels of work; freedom of choice of enrichment activities and intensive study of fewer, and often, new subjects. The effectiveness of arrangements to help students to overcome these difficulties should be evaluated.[6]

The old idea of 'we start them all at the same level and see who struggles'[7] is now discredited and is not desirable in any LRC in any school. To feel under pressure and to struggle are the last feelings that we want to be associated with learning and libraries.

This newly updated and thoroughly revised Guideline will consider the many issues surrounding library induction for newcomers and also transition arrangements for other people across the school.

It will look in particular at:

- induction for the new intake year and late entrants

- issues of transition for established students moving to 14+ and 16+ exams

- issues surrounding the often neglected area of the transition of students moving from school into higher education

- induction ideas for adults – teachers, support staff, Governors and of course parents – who need to become familiar with the role of the school library.

---

[3] p.15 Indicator ii Key Question 1. *Improve Your Library: A Self Evaluation Process for Secondary School Libraries and Resource Centres.* DfES, 2004.

[4] p.115 Inspecting schools. *Handbook for Inspecting Secondary Schools.* OFSTED, 2003.

[5] *Report on Standards and Quality in Primary and Secondary Schools in Scotland.* January 2002.

[6] p.116 Inspecting schools. *Op cit.*

[7] Quote from an article 'Thrown in at the deep end', *TES* 8 January 1999, referring to a report from OFSTED.

It will include a wide range of case studies from school library staff who are passionate to improve induction and transition arrangements in their libraries.

It will refer to some of the recent curriculum thinking and material now available about induction from OFSTED and the DCSF and the education services of other countries in the UK. It will suggest strategies that LRC staff can use to organise effective induction and transition for everyone who needs to use the library and its services, or to learn about the ways in which the library and its services can support and enhance their new courses in school.

Transfer of pupils between schools (and the ensuing induction programme) takes place at differing ages in different education authorities and schools across the UK. Most transfers take place at 11+ years, but 12+, 13+ and 14+ transfer is not uncommon. This publication focuses mainly on transfer at the 11+ stage. Many of the outlined strategies and activities can be adapted for those who transfer at a later date. Many students also move to new schools and colleges at the 16+ stage.

The Wider Picture of Primary–Secondary Transfer

For many years the governments of the four home countries have given thought to the importance of transfer between primary and secondary schooling, especially where it relates to maintaining curriculum development and personal pupil achievement. Part of the rationale behind England's National Curriculum was to streamline curriculum continuity between the primary and secondary phases. Educational research, inspection reports and government advice to schools have focused on this issue especially in the last decade – essentially because government officials have felt that transition arrangements needed improvement if the drive towards raising standards is to continue.

Nearly a decade ago the OFSTED report *Changing Schools* quoted:

All schools involved in the survey recognized the need to improve continuity and progression, but few of them were giving sufficient priority to this task.[8]

In the same report the inspectors also noted:

Secondary schools were not building well enough on what their new pupils had achieved in English and mathematics in Year 6 and they had not set targets for improving pupils attainment during year 7.

In December 2005 OFSTED again commented:

- *Transition (continuity of learning) remains unsatisfactory in nearly a quarter of schools*

- *Where transition is best secondary schools use teacher exchanges, locally planned bridging units and (crucially for school library staff) build on primary school reading records*

- *Good transition relies on the prompt, accurate and complete transfer of data from primary schools.*

In a DCSF report of 2008[9] the message is reinforced:

Every transfer between schools or transition between key stages and year groups is a potential barrier to progress. Where transfers and transitions are at their strongest the social, emotional, curricular and pedagogical aspect of learning are managed in order to enable pupils to remain engaged with, and have control of, their learning.

---

[8] OFSTED. *Changing Schools*. HMI 507. July 2002.
[9] DCSF *Strengthening transfers and transitions. Partnerships for progress.* Ref. 0083-2008PDF-EN01.

This prompt also gives a similar message:

> Too little regard appears to be paid by many secondary schools to the reliable information on primary children's academic progress that now exists.[10]

There is similar focus elsewhere.

The TES (Scotland) reports:

> Close working between teachers is the key to pupils' successful transition in Scotland... three initiatives which targeted the dip in performance between primary and secondary have delivered some marked improvements.[11]

Again, in Northern Ireland, *Statutory Curriculum at Key Stage 3: Rationale and Detail* notes:

> Post primary teachers are encouraged to liaise with feeder primary schools to ascertain the focus of children's work, particularly in years 6 and 7.[12]

Wales has gone one step further in The Transition from Primary to Secondary School (Wales) regulations 2006. Regulation 5(7) states that the Transition Agreements should contain:

> 2. A description of how continuity of curriculum planning will be achieved from feeder primary schools to the secondary school
>
> 3. A description of how continuity in teaching and learning methods will be achieved in transition
>
> 4. A description of how consistency in the assessment, monitoring and tracking of pupils' progress will be achieved in transition.[13]

Across the board we all want more effective transition arrangements for our new students arriving in secondary school, none more so than school library staff who are usually overlooked in official induction and transition paperwork and whose important role in the induction and transfer process is rarely mentioned.

---

[10] *The Independent Review of the Primary Curriculum.* Sir Jim Rose. Ref. PPAPG/D35(3931)/1208/13. December 2008. Available from http://publications.teachernet.gov.uk

[11] *TES Scotland.* 26 January 2007.

[12] Section 2.4. p22. Available at: http://www.nicurriculum.org.uk/docs/key_stage_3/statutory_curriculum_ks3.pdf

[13] Welsh Statutory Instrument 2006 No520 (W64) ISBN 011091290X.

New Intake Induction – Key Thoughts

Initially, as you consider issues of transition and induction, it is quite useful to consider your introduction to your LRC post – how you benefited or didn't as the case may be. What lessons can be learned?

Most school librarians who have the time and resources rightly focus their energy and attention to the new intake students. Eager eyed and curious, as they are, more than a few of these young students will perhaps never have had an opportunity to use an effective 21st-century library. If they are very unlucky they may live beyond the reaches of the local library service and their primary school may only have been able to provide a few rather poorly organised and maintained bookshelves as a whole school library or even simply a series of 'book corners'. These new intake pupils may have never thought about the role and purpose of a school library, its curriculum function, its potential for promoting reading for pleasure, its organization and its management. If they are very unlucky indeed they may never have had the opportunity to borrow a book from a library – after all some primary schools still don't feel able to lend out books and other resources.

Secondary school library staff may have to start from the very beginning and even if the new students are library familiar, yours may well be the biggest and grandest that they have ever seen.

If we are realistic, the LRC and LRC induction doesn't usually take a high priority in the minds of most students soon to join 'big school' or those who have already just crossed the divide. They are much more concerned with immediate routines and procedures – school size and layout, new subjects, their teachers and teaching methods, moving between lessons, new uniform, homework, lunch arrangement, the toilets, travel and transport and their new low status and the often talked about threat of bullying. The myth – 'the building is cavernous, the teachers terrifying and the older children push your head down the toilet'[14] – isn't true, but myths are sometimes hard to dispel and tend to focus the young mind other than on the library or LRC.

The LRC is likely to come near the end of their list although it will often be at the forefront of school librarians' thinking and planning, certainly during the late summer term and in the early autumn.

One key aspect of induction, but certainly not the only one for these students, is **familiarization** with the library and its services and the vast majority of school librarians who have the time and support to carry out an induction programme focus on this obvious aspect.

It is however equally important to give a sharp focus to **continuity** in curriculum and in reader development – aspects that are sometimes forgotten in the rush to familiarise new pupils with library layout and generally accepted rules and procedures. It is really useful to have a general

[14] Quote from an article 'Shock of the new school', TES, 3 September 1999.

understanding of the primary school curriculum, particularly for Years 5 and 6, and to have an understanding of the literacy objectives (especially those relating to Research and Study Skills) for those specific years. Test yourself on your knowledge of these objectives – see Appendices 1a and 1b. Do get yourself a copy of the Primary Framework for literacy and mathematics from the DCSF to use as a reference.

It is also very important not to confuse a welcome and a short induction programme with a series of information literacy skills sessions that consider issues usually better dealt with in a real curriculum context with a teacher-LRC partnership.

> *'An induction is only intended as a prelude. It is rather like removing the lid from a box of chocolates and feasting your eyes on the contents – to try out all the flavours and distinguish between the hard and soft centres takes time and to reach the second layer takes longer still.'*[15]

Everyone across the school is doing their best to appear friendly and welcoming. They are attempting to make a positive impact on these new 'customers' who with their parents have selected the school and what it offers. It is essential then that the LRC induction has impact and relevance and also a real curriculum interest and focus. From the beginning of their new school careers it is really useful if these pupils see the librarian's curriculum knowledge, interest and enthusiasm and his/her relevance to their prior and future learning.

Library induction for the new intake students:

- welcomes them
- motivates them
- introduces them to...
    - The big, impressive and to them, new library. You can see all its faults, but it may well be the largest and most impressive library these young people have yet experienced.
    - All the exciting resources just waiting to be used for curriculum support and wider personal interests.
    - The cheerful, knowledgeable, approachable and helpful staff (that's you and your helpers!).
    - The very basic procedures needed to get them started using the resources and feeling comfortable there.

---

[15] Claire Drury 'How to Win Friends' article in the *Library Association Record*. June 1996.

Leave Dewey, alphabetical order, internet search skills, skimming and scanning, detecting bias, note taking, plagiarism etc. until later. Focus on the immediate welcome to motivate your new students. Induction should give them confidence and encourage them to return and enjoy the LRC and all it has to offer. They don't need to overload on names, systems and procedures at this early stage.

Although the induction period is relatively short in terms of the whole school year, minds are soon made up and attitudes formed. The marketing and promotional opportunities provided in the opening few weeks are enormous. First impressions usually last the longest.

'Our new library's really cool, Mum, and the librarian is great too'[16] is the message we need to know is being repeated in homes up and down the land at the beginning of the new school year.

It is essential to plan induction effectively and use strategies that demonstrate the importance of the LRC. Successful induction will give your new students the information and the confidence they need to see the LRC as a place of enjoyment, a place for private reading, browsing and relaxing as well as a vital support for school work, a key source of information for school and for developing their own interests. They may not have understood that message in their primary/middle school.

---

[16] Quote heard by the author some years ago.

Getting Started

The potential of the primary–secondary liaison programme

> *Nothing beats getting in the car, going down the road to your partner schools and actually having a look around and a chat with the Head, teachers, library coordinator and children about their library, reading and information literacy.*
>
> *Staying to join in or run a session doubles the value of the visit and should give you a real insight into their policies, practices, attitudes and knowledge.*[17]

The best place to start the induction process is in the partner (feeder) schools. Some LRC staff can't manage this – and clearly it's easier if you have a small number of partner schools who are cooperative. If you have a large number of schools to visit then start with those that send you most students. Try to organize a two or three year cycle of visits.

Schools and circumstances differ but all secondary schools have built partnerships with their neighbouring primaries and for many years the Government has positively encouraged an official interchange of staff, reciprocal visits and joint curriculum activities. Talk with your own teaching colleagues involved in this liaison. If you can join one of these induction programmes and become part of the school's induction team so much the better for the librarian and library status.

If you have a large number of partner schools then gather data about them – their environment, their use, their staff. It is always useful to have the following details:

- the name of the person with a library responsibility
- do they use their SLS?
- do they lend books and other resources to their pupils?
- do they organise their non-fiction resources in Dewey order?
- do they use library helpers?
- do they run bookclubs/author events?
- do they have a library management system?
- do they have internet access in the library?
- do they have other hard copy non-book resources?

---

[17] Geoff Dubber, Induction/Transition session PowerPoint slide.

- do they organise any formal information skills teaching with a library focus?
- can they provide – or can you take – some photos of their library environment?

If you can't do this through visits, then consider other means.

There will of course be some political issues when venturing beyond your own library, even though the benefits for you, LRC familiarisation and the pupils are clear.

The partner schools may possibly query your visit, especially if the children are revising hard for SATs! The best time to go is either well before or just after Y6 exam time. Remember too that the primary school staff may be quite possessive of their youngsters at this stage, until they have real confidence in you, your expertise and professionalism. They may feel besieged by visitors. The parents of the children may have opted for a different school too and not yours and of course what is happening back at your library if you are a one person band?

The DCSF has given much thought to induction/transition and their list of ideas for induction interchange between the primary and secondary sectors is impressive:[18]

- Meet with primary schools to agree additional data
- Visit partner schools
- Meet with Y6 teachers to analyse test scripts
- Use visits during the summer term to identify suitable Y7 curriculum targets
- Interview each pupil at their primary school
- Gather information about gifted and talented pupils
- Establish an effective pupil tracking system
- Identify particular pupils (Level 3) who would benefit from an intervention programme (e.g. Gifted and Talented programme)
- Arrange visits to the new school and experience some teaching
- Exchange teachers KS2 and KS3.

Further ideas include:

- Feedback provided to primary schools on progress

---

[18] Ideas taken from *A Condensed Key Stage 3 Curriculum: Improving Key Stage 2 to Key Stage 3 Transfer*. DCSF Ref. 0003-2006DOC-EN. Available at http://nationalstrategies.standards.dcsf.gov.uk/node/154536

- Non-teaching staff to be fully involved (does that include library staff, I ask?)
- Quality information provided to parents
- Parent and pupil guides for new entrants
- Joint social events for Y6 / Y7 students
- Pupil peer mentoring
- Data effectively used across the school
- Setting of attainment targets
- Cross-phase teaching
- Joint projects and cross-phase activities
- Catch up programmes in Y7, especially for literacy
- Common language for discussing learning
- Joint training of staff
- Pupils developing a learning portfolio – Y6 to Y7.

Now if this comprehensive list is good enough for teachers to seriously consider as strategies for transition and raising attainment then it's equally good enough to be adapted for and used by library staff.

See the checklists for other ideas – Appendices 2a and 2b to help your thinking.

It may also be useful to create your own LRC focused links – emails, website use, blogs, conferencing, are all possible given some support, energy and time. Consider creating a specific reading award too – see the Southwark Book Award (Case Study 4) as a classic and successful example of encouraging Y6 – Y7 interaction within a book and library context.

Some librarians also link up with their primary partners through CILIP's Carnegie and Kate Greenaway Book Award shadowing scheme.[19] This school focuses on the Kate Greenaway Award:

> 'we work with the Y5 class in the local primary school and a Y7 top stream class... I encourage the (primary) teacher to get the Y5 children to take books home to read to younger siblings or read them to younger primary pupils and to engage with the shadowing site... we link with the English and Art Departments getting the Y7 pupils to discuss the books, take them home for family reading and put reviews onto the shadowing site.

---

[19] http://www.carnegiegreenaway.org.uk/

We encourage them to make an artistic response... and we then invite in an illustrator to take sessions with each class. We finish off the day by getting the two classes together for a debate about the books and a vote on which one should win'.[20]

The primary schools may like to visit you.

Pupils from primary schools visit us – for drama workshops linked to the Southwark Book Award, library skills lessons, after school book clubs, shared Bookweek events etc. This is obviously by far the easier option as the onus is on the primary school to do risk assessments, permission letters, organize helpers/parents to accompany children. I usually just send out a letter to each school's Head and/or the relevant Year Group teacher with my proposal and follow up with a phonecall. I have a list of names of kids coming, sort out refreshment breaks... and usually the visits last 1–2 hours at the most.[21]

---

[20] Karen Hans, librarian at St.-Martin-in-the-Fields High School for Girls.
[21] Quote from Laura Taylor, Librarian, City of London Academy – see Case Study 4.

The LRC Profile/Questionnaire

One of the best ways of finding out about the library experiences and reading/information interests of your new students en masse is to invite them to complete a simple questionnaire. This needs to be done in a relaxed but formal setting. Pupils may need lots of time and help to provide useful answers – especially those with poor reading and writing skills. Ideally it can be done as part of the primary–secondary liaison programme activities with help from their existing class teacher and support staff

> *I find using a questionnaire to find out about them really useful. It takes time to sort through all their responses but it tells me so much more about individuals than I would otherwise learn.*

If it cannot be completed at that stage then use it during the September induction session(s), although September is a little late if you're to have any time to reflect on their answers and assemble impressions or actual data. The answers you receive will, at their simplest, inform you of the attitudes and experiences of your new students.

These answers can:

- inform displays – favourite authors, books etc
- provide interesting statistics – reading habits and book buying, use of local library, ICT use – these can be displayed graphically and also used for base line assessment as part of the LRC's 'value added' contribution to learning
- provide valuable information about individuals – were they library helpers in their previous school?
- show differences between partner schools and their libraries
- inform your induction messages and session(s).

See Appendix 3 for a sample student questionnaire.

Although enormously valuable, beware that all answers may not be entirely accurate. Experience shows that occasionally students will provide the answer they think you expect rather than that ones you really want.

Curriculum and Reading Continuity

Curriculum continuity is essential if the library is to help to raise achievement, develop and promote its curriculum role, and maintain a high profile in the school's induction activities. It is important for library staff to become familiar with the skills levels, curriculum knowledge and experiences of their new intake customers. Becoming acquainted with the primary English curriculum and Y6 and also Y7 teaching objectives in particular is really helpful.[22] It immediately gives you curriculum leverage with the new and impressionable students and demonstrates to them that you support learning and enables useful dialogue with your school's induction/transition team.

My advice is to keep these listed objectives for easy reference – not only will they inform your induction activities and discussions, but can usefully act as a starting point for any information literacy work carried out within a curriculum context with your newcomers once induction is completed.

Transition units

These are units of work produced to be used by the Y6s at the end of the summer term and completed during their first few weeks in secondary school. The ones produced by the government are now aging rapidly. Many school partnerships have created their own transition units – usually with a specific subject focus – there will be many opportunities for school library staff to contribute to this work. The Government ones were produced in 2002. The two English units 'Authors' and 'Texts' were popular with some schools. They focus on basic literacy work rather than wider use of research skills or library use and the potential role for the library is ignored. The texts used include works by authors such as Michael Morpurgo (*Butterfly Lion, Kensuke's Kingdom, The Dancing Bear* etc.) Jacqueline Wilson (*The Suitcase Kid*) and Anne Fine (*Bad Dreams*).

These units can be found at
http://nationalstrategies.standards.dcsf.gov.uk/node/104267

If you and your school are keen on transition work of this type then LRC and wider curriculum partnerships could usefully focus on

- An island study with *Kensuke's Kingdom*
- World War One and the *Butterfly Lion*
- Induction experiences and *Bad Dreams*
- Family difficulties and *The Suitcase Kid*
- Displays of books by these authors.

---

[22] For those in state schools in England, do have a look at *The Primary Framework for Literacy and Mathematics*. DFES, 2006. 1-84478-794-X Ref. 02011-2206BOK-EN. DFES-03876-2006.

In Scotland the Curriculum for Excellence clearly states:

> 'The transition from primary school should be smooth and offer progression and continuity of learning and teaching approaches...it is important that young people experience a suitable, challenging gradient of progression during this period, maintaining progress from the achievements in their primary school...'

The Scottish Building Bridges in Literacy P6 – S2 project from 2003 produced some interesting work, especially notable for library staff is the Aberdeenshire Reading Detectives project in which Kemnay Academy worked with one of its partners, Alehousewells Primary School.

In Welsh schools the emphasis on curriculum continuity and transition bridging units is equally important. An interesting example of transition cooperation between Nantwell Church in Wales Primary School and Llandrindod High School is quoted in *TES Cymru* 20 May 2005.[23]

Reading habits

What can you find out about their reading habits, their breadth and depth of reading?

The National Literacy Trust has developed a 'Reading School' audit, part of which includes a focus on primary/secondary links:

- Specific ideas are used to ease transition, e.g. Y6 pupils send suggested holiday reads to their new school for display on their entry to Y7.
- Regular initiatives aid transition – for example, visits by Y7 and older pupils for reading activities.
- School develops a reading for pleasure strategy with feeder primary schools.

See more ideas on the Reading Connects website.[24]

Use the highly popular Summer Reading Challenge, from The Reading Agency, as a way to link with primary partner schools.

> *This year we experimented further using the Summer Reading Challenge (SCR) to develop and maintain links between public libraries and secondary schools and their primary feeder schools to support transition children. ...We produced materials that were successful in extending the appeal of the Challenge to the older 11+ age range. 96% of libraries were involved , 690,000 children took part in the SRC – 58% of them completed the full Challenge by reading 6 books over the summer.*[25]

---

[23] http://www.tes.co.uk/article.aspx?storycode=2105507
[24] http://www.readingconnects.org.uk
[25] Report. The Summer Reading Challenge 2008.

Follow up with certificates and an award ceremony. This provides continuity not only between schools but also develops partnerships with the local library service.

Library experiences

What can you find out about the general library experiences of these pupils – their use of their existing school library (if there is one) and the local library?

Organise them in pairs or small groups to interview and perhaps video each other about their library experiences and reading interests and habits.

What do they know about the information network beyond school? – specialist library collections, archives, museums etc.

What can you find out about their use and experiences of using the Internet and ICT in general for information handling?

> *We do 'Fastest Fingers' PowerPoints where students are shown a question on the interactive whiteboard and the first to find the answer puts up a hand and wins a 'prize'. This enables us to see how they choose keywords, select their search engines and strategies and combine terms – can be great fun depending on the questions!*[26]

Consider giving every incoming student a brief interview to assess their information literacy skills so you can be aware of their personal level.[27]

The information you glean will guide the context and to an extent the content and tone of your induction. They probably know less than you think they might and applying what they do know in a completely fresh setting of the new school may well be difficult for them.

---

[26] Eileen Armstrong, Cramlington Learning Village, Northumberland.
[27] Lynn Barrett, previously Librarian at Dixons CTC, has done this very effectively.

Impress the New Parents/Carers

First impressions always count and how will this curious and hopefully eager group first learn about your library, your curriculum input and your general profile and expertise?

After all in a survey in early 2009[28] parents were asked their view of what made an ideal education and 74% said a good library was key (along with good discipline, regular contact with parents and a broad range of abilities, cultures and background).

They will almost certainly have explored the school website and browsed the school's prospectus before considering a school visit so get in early with your parents' induction strategy.

Opening one magazine I found:

> *How to choose a school: Do pay a visit to the library to check on the range and suitability of books and the extent of Internet access but DON'T be impressed by rows of neatly stacked (unused) volumes. Lots of dog-eared, recently published books are usually a sign of a productive library.*[29]

Does your school produce glossy literature for prospective/new parents and carers? Most do. It puts the school in the best possible light, outlining facilities, policies, the curriculum and student successes in a range of fields, academic, sporting and cultural. Usually many curriculum subjects have a mention – but what about the LRC and its contribution to learning? You support the learning and teaching needs of everyone across the school – the LRC should have a section to itself. The first understanding for the prospective or new parents of the LRC and its role and importance may well be through this literature.

Consider:

- the production schedule for this new material
- staff responsible for its production
- the house style
- space allocated to specific subjects and items
- the wording you can add about the LRC and its contribution to raising attainment.

Put together your contribution, include quotes from new intake students, show photographs of you in action or a montage of photos, feature any recent author visits and generally show the library as a vibrant and

---

[28] An Ipsos MORI poll quoted in *The Observer*, 22 March 2009.
[29] *Living Edge* magazine (Cheshire) September 2006, p111.

motivational area. Try not to include too may plain facts and figures – it is more about what the library contributes to raising achievement than highlighting opening hours, book numbers or ICT usage. Discuss it with your line manager and have it ready for inclusion, even if nobody thought to ask you.

Open the library at appropriate Parents' Evenings and Open Days. Bear in mind the following points:

- What professional image do you hope to give?

- What range of resources will you show in use?

- How will the library look active and curriculum focused?

- What will be the main messages about learning and reading that you provide? Use quotes from students and self-evaluation data in some of your displays, e.g. *'We loaned 25,000 books last year, an increase of 25% from the previous year, 42 students regularly attend our Homework Club'* — it looks impressive!

- What will you say about Gifted and Talented students and those with Special Needs?

- What handouts will you have available – a special one just for the parents?

- Will you create a family book quiz too? – with prizes of course

- What other freebies will you offer – bookmarks, stickers, pens with the LRC logo?

- What will the parents/carers have been told about the LRC by siblings already?

Whatever you manage to do with your limited resources, talk curriculum, reading and students.

Keep Consulting!

Make a point of consulting with:

The **Year Head/Pastoral Care Staff /Head of Learning Support** responsible for liaison with the primary schools and new intake students to learn about

- predicted numbers
- students' ability levels. Identifying students with particular academic or social needs is important at this stage
- details of the new tutor and teaching groups
- the July Induction Day(s) programme to negotiate the library's role in this event
- the arrangements for the new Parents' Evening/Open Day that usually accompanies the Induction Day.

Senior Managers and Heads of Faculty/Department to arrange:

- dates and times for library induction sessions
- plans for library-based work that will be carried out by the new students as part of their curriculum work in the forthcoming Autumn term. This will make the best use of any initial induction by developing library use in a curriculum context. Departments will need to book time in the library for students so that teachers can work closely with library staff to develop effective information handling skills.

Local public library services and your Schools Library Service to find out about the induction programmes used or recommended by them. If most of the new intake students coming to your school have experienced such programmes, it will be useful for you know about them. Your own planned activities can refer back to these.

- When will you take your new intake down to the local library for a talk and tour?

The Summer Term Induction Event

During the event

What's in the day's programme? A tour of the school, an exciting activity or two on the sports field or the science lab...? A meeting with their new tutor and tutor group are the essential recipe for the visit, but what about the LRC? Is it a walk through or round or can you have them for longer?

- How long can you have with them?
- How many will visit you – in a specific group? during the day?
- What will you do with them?
- What message do you want them to take away?

It may be just a quick walk round – and this could be their first look into the LRC – but how will they remember it and how will they remember you?

Try to avoid this difficult situation:

'... I have been told at 08:30 this morning that I have 60 Yr6 kids coming to the library after lunch today for 35 mins. They won't be able to sit at tables as they just won't fit in, so any written or colouring work is out the question. Also I don't have any other staff with me.'

More hopeful and with more potential is:

'I always work with our primary children when they come into school for our Primary Week.'

Induction needs impact!

If only the walk through/walk around is possible then the other links will be all the more important.

If possible find time for some of these:

- Quizzes and competitions – offer small prizes. LRC badges, pencils etc.
- A student profile/questionnaire
- Treasure hunts and locator maps
- Browsing the LRC ICT
- Question and answer sessions
- Reading them a story – how about one with a library context? Try extracts from Eoin Colfer's *The Legend of Spud Murphy*[30] but remember to read the end of the story otherwise the librarian is seen as a child-eating monster!

---

[30] Published by Puffin, 2004. ISBN 978 0 141 38016 2.

If you have the minimum of time try these:

- Wear a big badge with your name on it and a simple message about you, your role or the importance of books/reading
- Wear some bright or unusual clothes for the day
- Display a large message for them or statistics about the LRC to read as they pass through
- Have some interesting music playing during their visit
- Show them something really interesting about the LRC – perhaps your most expensive/biggest/smallest/oldest resource and tell them you'll remind them of it when you see them again at the start of the next term.

See **Appendix 4** for a possible Top Twenty Induction Activities.

Meet the Parents

During the evening when the parents are invited:

- Wear the same badge you wore throughout the day
- Play the same music
- Display the same messages/statistics
- Invite the parents to have a go at the same quizzes or competitions their children tried during the day, perhaps to be completed later with their children. Offer small prizes!

The impact you make is important – you want the parents to support you and your work once their children are part of the school and using the LRC on a daily basis for study and leisure reading. Behaviour, overdues etc will become less of a challenge. Your professionalism is more likely to be accepted by the students.

Planning the Autumn Term Session(s)

Many factors affect the nature, style and organisation of induction sessions – especially your enthusiasm, personality, experience, prior planning and the entire ethos of the LRC itself.

Remember there is no perfect induction session or programme.

Sessions should be:

- planned and introduced by LRC staff
- planned as a special timetabled arrangement, preferably with sessions of 1–2 hours
- carried out jointly by LRC staff and also the tutors or relevant curriculum staff who would normally be teaching the students at that time. At this early stage without knowing names, experiences and abilities the greater the number of adults that you can have for these sessions the better.

Preparation

1. Think yourself into the role of a new student – what would you want to know?

- location
- opening times
- staff names and responsibilities
- the library layout – use of signs and guiding
- methods of borrowing and returning books and other resources
- ways to book and use ICT equipment, software and the photocopier
- the range of resources, their organisation and their location
- essential rules and regulations – probably about conduct and ways of dealing with coats and bags
- that the LRC is 'the place to go' for information to answer questions, for research, for ideas and for tapping into the knowledge and experience of the wider information world.

2. Clarify the aims of the session and share them with the students – it's always good practice.

I've had more thoughts on the induction programme, especially sharing the aims of it with the pupils, common sense really. I will... put up a poster with the following checklist:

> *By the end of this time in the LRC you should be able to:*
> *Understand what the LRC is for*
> *Find your way around the LRC*
> *Know where fiction and non-fiction books are kept*
> *Know how to find a fiction book*
> *Know how to find a non fiction book*
> *Know what the Look Up Point is for*
> *Understand when you can use the LRC*

and then discuss it at the beginning and end of each session.

How long will it take to cover this issue? Is one longer session better than two shorter ones? Remember that every newcomer will need time and space to explore and enjoy the exciting and attractive range of resources that the LRC has to offer and the time and confidence to borrow what they choose. A hurried and stressful atmosphere at this stage can do more harm than good.

3. What do you need to know about the new students?

- their names and tutor group allocations
- their library knowledge, attitudes and experiences
- information about students with Special Educational Needs.

In some schools LRC staff still find this information about Special Needs hard to obtain. Don't give up. Explain why you need it. If you are to really support these students it is most important that you can identify them and learn of their specific difficulties – either physical or learning.

> *'This has helped me no end when working with deaf students and those with ADHD, Aspergers Syndrome and one with Tourette's Disorder – if I hadn't know I would probably have told him off for shouting out !'*[31]

---

[31] Claire Larson

4. Plan the activities

How about using any of these?

- compile answers in a booklet the students take away

- complete a library locator map – to vary this a little, take some photographs and turn them into either digital[32] or glossy/hardboard backed jigsaw puzzles for the students to use

- use the school/library 'Steps to learning' framework as a card sort activity[33]

- answer quizzes to show or reinforce alphabetical or Dewey order (many commercial examples available)

- answer quizzes about the library and its resources – these could be ICT based

- watch an in-house DVD about the library and its use

- try out the library's computerized catalogue/issue system

- listen to some extracts of favourite and familiar books or short stories

- browse the resources to become familiar with their variety and use (this can also be achieved by organizing small group 'treasure hunts')

- borrow some books, audio books, DVDs or other resources

- take part in a question and answer session

- complete the LRC profile/questionnaire if not done so previously (see Appendix 3)

- use the highly popular Reading Game available from Carel Press[34]

- carry out a subject-specific activity planned with a department or faculty

- take part in team quizzes that involve simple general knowledge and trivia, with answers that can be found easily from books on the library shelves or ICT

- create a poster about interesting information they discover

- design a 'library of the future' leaflet or poster.

---

[32] See an example at http://www.ecademy.com/module.php?mod=list&lid=104796
[33] See SLA Guideline – *Information Matters: Developing Information Literacy Skills Through the Secondary School LRC*. pp22-23 and pp50-53.
[34] http://www.carelpress.co.uk

Is it worth putting some of the materials onto your VLE or library webpages?

Library staff in the Newman Library at Brooke Weston College, Northamptonshire, have uploaded their induction booklets for the new intake year and also the Y12s onto their webpages.[35]

Remember – *Induction needs to be lively, relaxed and have impact.*

5. Plan the working groups

Groups/classes coming to the LRC for induction usually sit around the library in random or friendship groups for activities. This may be useful, but it may be difficult for those with Special Needs or those with above average library knowledge.

Invite the tutor or class teacher to organise the class into broad ability bands then ask him/her to work along side those who appear to need more help or maybe with those already familiar with the LRC and its workings. Differentiated material and specific support may benefit these students.

Setting up a number of workstations with different activities, perhaps five or six for the average class size and organising students to rotate around these activities with a fixed amount of time for each one may be more interesting and easier to organise than having all the students simultaneously carrying out the same activities.

6. Plan the timing

Which is better? What can you negotiate because you know what you want and why you want it?

- The drip feed process of a number of timetabled lessons per week/fortnight?
- Block booking a class for a whole morning or afternoon and 'blitzing' them with a lively and memorable session?

How about starting with a short film made by older students about the LRC and its work? This will often raise interest, especially if the newcomers see and hear students in older years that they know already.

If pushed for time this video could be shown by tutors as a warm up for the library based induction sessions.

A one-off session or two short ones are more likely to send students rushing home to tell parents and carers about the wonderful LRC and library staff,

---

[35] http://www.brookeweston.org/Learning/Library/Inductions.aspx

the wonderful books and resources they are able to borrow, and the colourful and interesting leaflets, bookmarks or badges they have been given.

Finish the initial induction quickly and then get the students into the LRC, learning to use the resources as they need them in a curriculum context.

> *'Within the first two weeks of term, all twelve Yr 7 forms had visited the library for their induction. Pupils were now familiar with the location and layout of the library, they had met the librarian and Wordsworth (the library mascot), had some understanding of the different types of books in the library and how they were organised...'*[36]

Provide a library mascot (or even two). If suitably chosen it can provide a focus for interest and enjoyment.

7. Prepare materials

Create, photocopy, label and file all materials that will be needed for the forthcoming sessions.

8. Inform all participants

Distribute the induction programme and timetable to the senior management team, heads of department, the teaching staff and other colleagues involved and, of course, to student librarians. It is especially important to get the support and commitment of teaching staff, so don't try to impress them by surprising them with your brilliant session. Make sure they know as much about it as possible first. They are then more likely to be interested and supportive.

---

[36] *Are You Sitting Comfortably?* Marie Hewitt and Anne Taylor, Paignton Community College.

The Autumn Term

You've got them. They are your next group of important customers – they may be with you for the next five to seven years.

Now for the last stage of the induction programme

- You saw them in primary/middle school
- You have learnt of their LRC and literacy experiences
- Their names are now listed on your management system
- You have received details of their individual learning needs and any health problems
- They have completed a student profile
- You've seen some of their parents/carers
- They know the LRC is important – if induction is working effectively, many will have visited already, they and their parents/carers have seen it featured in the school's literature and heard about it from older siblings
- They are excited to borrow your amazing resources
- They want to make use of the LRC
- It should be all systems GO!

Final Checks

Make a final check of the arrangements made at the end of the summer term:

- The dates and times of each induction session
- The names and numbers of the new intake classes and the teaching and support staff who will accompany them and work with them during the sessions.

Don't be too dismayed if your plans have to be changed at this late stage. Keep positive and cheerful even when your flexibility is tested to the limit by inevitable juggling of staff, classes and rooms that takes place at the beginning of every school year.

Enthuse!

Carry out your induction programme with as much energy and enthusiasm as you can generate – remembering to wear your big badge again with your name and LRC slogan on it. This is especially important as you may be giving the same session many times, but for the students it is still their first time and they deserve to be impressed.

Special Needs

Don't forget the Special Needs students. Lots of them may already be suspicious of the LRC as it signifies 'reading' which to them may be difficult, 'boring', and sapping of self-confidence. They may be used to producing lots of unfinished work so anything you can do to give them tasks that they can complete will reap rewards. It is so much better working in small groups at this stage rather than being overwhelmed by solo tasks. It means activities can be finished and successful. Even so they may need a bit more time and reinforcement to finish the job and feel a sense of achievement.

Certificate

Don't forget the certificate!

Acknowledge success. Give a simple certificate to everyone who successfully completes the induction programme – everyone should do so if possible. This can improve motivation and self-esteem. Invite the class tutor or Head of Year to sign the certificate as well as adding your own signature. This will increase teaching staff's awareness of the induction programme, its aims and success. (See Appendix 5 for a sample certificate).

Make Space

Arrange to have the LRC closed for a few lunchtimes to all but the new intake – other classes in the school will not, in this early stage of the year, have done enough work to need to make much use of the library. This gives your newcomers the space and confidence to browse and borrow without the usual pressures of noise and crowds. Ask any new student – nothing is more off putting than finding the big noisy older ones in there first! Equally the older ones can be put off by so many newcomers 'invading their space'.

Follow up

Follow up the induction with library related curriculum work, targeting specific information skills with the librarian/LRC manager working in partnership with the teachers (see *Information Matters: Developing Information Literacy Skills through the Secondary School LRC*).

Later in the Autumn Term

Evaluate **Evaluate** the entire induction process and its timing.

Liaise with staff who were involved and ask their opinions. Try to evaluate the quality of what was achieved by asking students and staff:

- what they learned
- whether the lessons 'stuck'
- what they remember most
- what they enjoyed most
- whether or not they have they visited the LRC again (and if so for what reason?).

Discuss **Discuss** your conclusions with your line manager and obtain a commitment that the LRC can again feature in the primary-secondary liaison programme for the coming year and remember your new piece for the school prospectus.

Amend **Amend** the master copies of handouts/webpages/activities etc. in the light of comments and experience.

File **File** the completed student questionnaires for use later as circumstances allow.

Remember the Other New Students

'They always seem to get left out' is a frequent comment. New students frequently join the school in years other than Y7, Y10 and Y12. It is just as important to effectively welcome these newcomers to the LRC as all the others. Other students may well enter the school during the academic year. Often they will feel unsettled to change school at this stage in their school career and to have their friendship pattern and normal daily routines upset. The change may well have been enforced by changes in their family situation or by unhappiness in a previous school so anything the LRC can do to reduce the stress and ease the transition will be welcome.

Key issues

- How many of them are there?
- How do you find out about them and their previous LRC experiences? Check to find out if they still owe their previous school any LRC resources.
- How do they learn about the services you can offer? – handouts, leaflets, webpages.
- How well do they use the LRC?

Induction for this group will often be more ad-hoc with timing, but nevertheless structured as their numbers will be fewer.

- Alert school admin staff to provide you with details of these students at enrolment.
- Obtain further information from pastoral care staff.
- 'Round them up' on a regular basis during tutor time or during curriculum time and make sure that their induction is as clear and welcoming as that given to all the other newcomers.

Transition for the 14+ Examination Course Students

While concern over transition problems is focused on the move from primary to secondary school, it can be argued that there are issues of progression at each Key Stage. Schools need to be more aware of the prior experiences of pupils and of the teaching practices of the previous Key Stage.[37]

Many school library staff are now aware of the need for a further focus on the library and all it has to offer to the 14+ exam cohorts. Y10 (Fourth Year) induction can start in the summer term of Y9 (Third Year) as options choices will have been made and many schools push students to start exam courses early rather than risk the end of Y9 slump.

We both felt that Year 9 needed reminding about what the LRC has to offer and both agreed that GCSE coursework or controlled assessment can be a daunting prospect when tackled for the first time in Year 10 – hence this project... We ran an informal coursework clinic for them every lunchtime and it was good fun... we are able to introduce them to the topic files, the online newspapers and Essential Articles, all of which they will need in Years 10 and 11.

All these students should be familiar with the LRC already – the basic resources and their organisation, its procedures, code of practice and other regulations. Hopefully they have become regular users. They are, however, making a new beginning, moving up a stage, starting fresh courses, and in the last few week of Y9 or during the first few weeks of the Autumn Term they should be feeling enthusiastic and motivated.

Make sure that the LRC and its resources and contribution for learning feature in information sent home to parents and carers about 14+ courses. This will increase and reinforce LRC credibility at home and with the students. As with the new intake year information, concentrate on what the library contributes to learning (and in this case exam success) rather than provide lots of details about LRC provision and procedures.

- In the first instance concentrate on the forthcoming controlled assessment or coursework that they will be working on

- Know about their curriculum work – especially the changes to GCSE that are imminent and when coursework/controlled assessment units are organised – show them these on a yearly planner or on some webpages – another way in which the LRC can act as a reference point

- If they are starting out on one of the new Diploma courses, then talk about those too and the possibilities/expectations for project work

---

[37] Steer, Sir Alan (Chair). *Review of Pupil Behaviour: Interim Report.* 4 February 2009.

- Tell them about your out of hours study support clinics, study sessions or other strategies to help them with their new courses

- Straight from the horse's mouth! Organise one or more of your LRC student volunteers to do some of the talking for you

- Explain your exam/coursework resources – revision guides, past papers, bookmarks – real or virtual, listing useful resources for specific topics, overnight loan procedures for key resources etc. Perhaps offer them different borrowing arrangements from the younger students

- Outline any new curriculum or careers/guidance resources and materials now available to them as they start their all important exam courses

- Offer a 'refresher' on searching skills or note taking or the use of different search engines at a specific time, separate from the induction session

- Invite each of them to give you a list of subjects/options/coursework topics etc details to help you to provide a better service. You may have this available through the school database, but asking the students to complete a list especially for you in the LRC will give the right messages and show you mean business in your efforts to help them.

Clearly you cannot expect the same levels of interest, enthusiasm and commitment from students who have not used your expertise and facilities since Y7.

Sorting the Sixth – the 16+ Students

Let's face it, for many school library staff, so very busy at the start of the new academic year with newcomers lower down the school and new adults, sixth form induction isn't that much of a priority. Many LRC staff find difficulty getting the required curriculum time for any induction, but ignore them at your peril. We all know that Sixth Form induction really starts in Y7 and that their library and library staff experiences will colour their attitude to a large extent. Your professional standing and networking with the Sixth Form tutors and in particular the Head of Sixth will also be important. One complication that you may also face is a large influx of students from other schools who have joined your school for their Sixth Form experience. Another may be a shortage of Sixth Former study space, so the library space is often under intense pressure.

Sixth Formers in an LRC can be a dream or a disaster. They can easily become restless, unfocused, and even confrontational on occasions. They may abuse the ICT equipment and it can be a constant battle to keep them quiet and to prevent them from challenging the library rules. In other schools they can be a real influence for good – providing help when needed as an extra adult presence in the LRC. Their insights into current affairs, their general knowledge and offers of support can be refreshing and invigorating. To quote one librarian:

> *I would like to say that the huge pleasure I have from working with Sixth Form students keeps me sane. They assist with the Y7 and Y8 reading groups, they help with our homework club and they stand in for me when I attend meetings. I cannot imagine how I would manage without them.*

Whatever they are like they will probably benefit from some induction and they probably need focused but perhaps relaxed curriculum/skills advice from a very patient and professional librarian – that's you! Remember that this year's new Y12s will soon 'get the message' from last year's Y12s – the novelty of being in the Sixth Form can soon wear off.

Sixth Form inductions can vary enormously. For example:

- *One 45 min session. Groups of 15 – re-introducing the library, the OPAC and mention of on-line databases, using magazines and newspapers, mentioning library rules (again!), a mention of sites other than Google and a task to specific texts and subjects.*

- *Nine forms of about 20 students per class seen in rotation during the first two days of school. Up to 10% come from different schools – I do a card sorting activity on 'What the Library can do for Me', then I do a bit about the OPAC and keyword searching, Google advanced search, introduce Intute and cover some plagiarism and copyright issues.*

- *I provide an 'Introduction to the Library for Sixth Formers' leaflet that outlines the basics, opening hours, behaviour, layout, borrowing, fines, on-line services, ICT usage, music, Basic Dewey sections and becoming a student librarian. I also provide a sheet about AS/A2 study skills covering task planning, note taking and skimming and scanning, and remind them never to be afraid to ask for help.*

Why have a Sixth Form induction?

OFSTED have some clear views on the subject of Sixth Form induction/ transition:

The transition from KS4 to post compulsory education can bring difficulties for students. These include:

- *Settling into different work patterns*
- *Control over their own timetables and time*
- *Facing different levels of work*
- *Freedom of choice with subjects*
- *Intensive study of fewer, often new subjects*
- *The effectiveness of arrangements to help students to overcome these challenges should be evaluated.*[38]

It may well be a challenge to obtain the time from hard pressed subject staff or tutors so it's essential that it is well planned and effective and can be proved to make a difference. Clearly, use of the library should be an important part of the school's introduction to the Sixth Form and it provides a clear opportunity to:

- Promote the LRC as central to Sixth Form learning – using it effectively should help them to maximize their exam grades
- Find out about your new Sixth Form users.

If at all possible it needs to be relaxed, entertaining and memorable for all the right reasons – it isn't a rather tortuous journey through information literacy – much of that needs to come later in a curriculum context, after all as with younger students, induction is a welcome.

The planning

It will be important that these new 16+ students 'hit the floor running' as far as transition into the Sixth Form is concerned. Curriculum schedules are so tight that effective use of the LRC within the first two to three weeks of the new year is essential.

- There is little time for adjustment to the new curriculum demands
- Last year's 16 years old exam students are this year's Sixth Formers

---

[38] OFSTED, September 2003.

- They will probably continue much as they did last year – but with more personal study time and some of it almost certainly spent in the LRC

- As with the younger students, make sure the LRC's role and services appear in the handbook/leaflets/options information sent to prospective Sixth Formers and their parents/carers. This will help LRC credibility and maximize the chances of Sixth Form use. It could even bring in extra LRC funding if you can demonstrate the centrality of the LRC to Sixth Form learning and study opportunities.

- Make sure the LRC features in the relevant parents' open evening/open days.

This is a great opportunity to show your professionalism and the LRC's direct involvement with learning and exam work.

The same messages apply as with the 14+ exam students.

- Know your curriculum subjects, basic curriculum content, coursework content and demonstrate your knowledge to them. Perhaps create a data file of requirements for each major subject and have coursework and extended project requirements and timings listed – perhaps on a large wall mounted grid.

- Promote your resources as enthusiastically as you can. Impress them with the resources you have to help them with subject content and exam and study techniques:

  - book stock and ICT software/courseware for their new courses
  - more complex reference materials, statistics, maps, local area resources etc.
  - census data, geology maps and so on
  - examples of coursework done in previous years
  - syllabus information from the examination boards
  - copies of past exam papers
  - examination revision guides.

- Explain the study facilities now available to them and the extra support you can offer to this special user group – perhaps a specific time during the week when you plan to be available for 'study surgeries' to help them with more complex information needs and research/study problems when the LRC will be quieter.

- Explain the ways in which LRC staff use wider information networks to find copies of other books, articles, journals etc. to support their class and coursework.

- Outline some of the new information literacy skills they will be called upon to use – writing lengthy essays, citing sources etc. and outline any aids you have produced to support these skills, or perhaps as a taster, point them to the many HE web based tutorials that cover these skills.

- Alert them to the Higher Education and university prospectuses and careers information that you hold. Aspiration at this stage is important as it can provide and focus their motivation.

- If appropriate issue their new borrower's card/tickets.

You'll also need to explain to them some or all of the following:

- Use of library ICT – when and how, probably reinforcing the school's Approved User Policy

- Information about private study procedures – signing in, numbers allowed, movement around the library during private study

- Use when other classes are active in the library

- Noise levels – use for groups and paired working, or are you operating a solo working and silent study area?

- Food and drink issues

- Use of mobile phones, iPods, MP3s and games consoles etc

- Use of the photocopier.

Clearly you need to avoid a long list of 'don'ts', but some guidance given in a friendly and welcoming manner will be needed – maybe in poster form, in a series of positive photographs; or as a part of a 'helping us to help you' type leaflet; or as a card sort (match questions to answers) activity; or perhaps as information on either your LRC plasma screen or your library ICT screensaver and login requirements; after all these students have not yet used the LRC as Sixth Formers.

Also consider the information that library staff need to serve them effectively:

- Get them each to fill in a questionnaire for you about their studies and intended use of the LRC. Each person is a separate and important user of your service, so knowing their situation and aspirations is important – that will give you a good idea of the spread of subjects, numbers of students studying them, amount of non-curriculum time etc. Clearly you can obtain that information from other sources, but the psychological effect of completing details for you in the library could well be important.

- Consider using a Sixth Form Contract with them – see Appendix 6.

Plan your choice of strategy for delivering your key messages. Depending on the time you have available it will probably be a mixture of:

- Exhortation
- Lecture
- Question and Answer session
- PowerPoint session
- Group treasure hunt or quiz
- Card sort

and perhaps a piece of research to practise some specific skills.

Will you go for a generic induction carried out through tutor groups and with the tutor at the end of the summer term when they have finished their 16+ exams, or at the beginning of the new school year following results and course decisions?

Or perhaps you could carry out subject-specific induction carried out in smaller exam focused groups with departmental teachers.

Which seems more effective? What do other staff think? What are the views of the Head of the Sixth Form and heads of department? You may well end up with a mix and match strategy.

How will you deliver key messages?

Popular now with some school library staff is the Cephalonian Method.[39] It has proved a useful strategy when dealing with large numbers of students although smaller groups will usually produce more interactive participation. Created in 2002 for library induction for Y1 medical and biological students at Cardiff University by their enterprising library staff, it involves a mixture of colour, audience participation with the added interest of some music.

By splitting the induction session clearly into a number of sections, the library staff plant questions on colour coded cards in the audience – perhaps all those concerning private study could be of one colour, while procedures about borrowing resources could be another. The library staff then use a PowerPoint presentation and as appropriate ask the audience for a card of the relevant colour to be read out to everyone. The skill is to raise issues and provide answers in a light hearted manner – humour being used in both the question and the answer.

Initially the Cardiff librarians wanted their audience to consider use of the photocopier. The question became 'My mum has emailed me a photograph

---

[39] See http://www.sconul.ac.uk/publications/newsletter/32/2.rtf
also http://www.sconul.ac.uk/publications/newsletter/40/21.pdf

of Miguel, my pet iguana – where can I print out the photo?' The PowerPoint slide showed a picture of Miguel. The slides also included a range of humorous clipart.

Some librarians who have tried it think that it works well, others are a little less sure. It needs confidence on the part of the audience and the presenters and ethos is an important element here too.

As with LRC transition planned for 14+ students, make it lively, relevant and provide enough detail. Make sure they leave the session thinking that the LRC is vital to their studies. They should feel enthusiastic and a little excited about using it in a more grown up and advanced way for resources and for private study. After all, the next stop for many will be the impressive and sophisticated libraries of universities and colleges.

If possible arrange to work in partnership with subject teachers for some if not all of these sessions. Show that the LRC is central to the work of that subject and department and its exam successes.

Key messages about the LRC, its resources and policies can then be displayed and promoted through a range of giveaway bookmarks and leaflets, available on the counter, placed in issued books or shown on LRC webpages or on your plasma screen.

As one librarian told me:

> 'LRC 'reminders' are subject specific and consist of a 'guided tour' of relevant resource areas to small groups of 'A' Level/GNVQ students.'

> 'A Y12-13 general leaflet is now available and must be completed and returned to the LRC before a 6th Form user ticket is allocated.'

Preparing to Move On

Widening participation and fair access to higher education is a key theme for Government at the moment. We need more of our Sixth Formers to enter and stay in higher education in its multiplicity of forms. Many students in the Sixth Form will already be moving into Higher Education and making use of much larger, busier, complex and sophisticated libraries – but how prepared are they for this move? If there is time and opportunity it may be useful to consider building links with local colleges and universities – after all your students may feel comfortable and confident with using your resources and your school library – they may have used them for the last seven years, but what happens next? The step up can be confusing for a large minority of students and even intimidating for some of them. We are all well aware of the disturbing drop out rate from universities, as many as 20% in some institutions, and familiarisation with the library, related study skills and discussions about workloads and expectations will undoubtedly ease the cross over.

Recent comments from university students, school library staff and university library staff reflecting on library links between schools and universities include:

- [there were] none at all to my knowledge, library induction at uni was very difficult for me (student)

- I was very uncertain when I started at uni about how to use the library – I never went near it for ages and when I did I went with some friends. It was a different world to being at school where I had been spoon fed by teachers and I lazed around in the library! (student)

- I've had to do a lot of searching for books for her as she hasn't a clue about using the on-line library facility, resorting instead to Amazon in some cases – so she's in for a tutorial or two when she comes home! (school librarian talking about her daughter)

- As part of an extended essay in A Level Philosophy, I (and the teacher) take a group of students to Manchester Uni to undertake research. Before they go we do some preparation by checking the Uni catalogue – they have to find at least three titles they think will be relevant and we look at bibliographies and plagiarism. They have a talk, a demo of online resources and a tour from a uni librarian when we arrive and then they are left to locate books and on-line information. The boys are on the whole quite impressed by the Uni library, its scale/size (school librarian)

- We offer tours to a couple of small groups, usually A Level students interested in how a university library works... nothing very systematic or comprehensive (university librarian)

- We don't do anything proactively (haven't the staff capacity) but try to be helpful if we are contacted by schools – usually it's the teachers (university librarian)

- I'm not aware that any of our staff go out to schools.. I think there is lots of potential for us collectively to do more. (university librarian)

Suggested strategies:

- Talk with your senior management/leadership team and Head of Sixth Form to discuss existing links and the potential for helping the school, and raising aspiration and motivation

- Make contact with the library staff at your local university/Higher Education Institution (HEI) to find out if they have the capacity and staffing to consider links

- Ask for a library tour yourself and perhaps the head of Sixth Form to consider the potential

- Consider how you personally would feel transferring from your own library to studying in this one

- Take some photographs of its environment and resources to make a display or use digitally in your own library

- Work with the Head of Sixth Form to consider the similarities and differences between the two libraries – how does your own library mirror and support the ethos and work of the HEI library? – does the school need to give your own Sixth Form students a more effective approach to learning and library use?

- Talk to interested subject teachers – especially those whose students are doing extended essays and similar work about the potential

- Organise a research visit – linked to using the resources, hard copy or on-line databases

- Although few of your own students may actually be studying at that particular establishment consider inviting HEI library staff back into your school to discuss transition issues – library induction during Fresher Week, the range of task set to students during their first term, information literacy issues in general – and use of the library with your students

- *'All but two freshers in the group failed their first module as they didn't properly reference their sources'* was a comment that I heard recently

- Organise your students, perhaps working with an ex-student from your school at the HEI to create a presentation about the library and its work.

Although time is short and resources and staffing limited, this could well be an area for development over the coming months and years as library staff work hard to help to raise school attainment and bring equality of access to higher education.

Adults Only

As part of staff induction we provide a series of relaxed after school sessions, over a cup of coffee, for all new staff. We encourage teaching and support staff to attend these sessions and cover all aspects of school life during the term with a different speaker each time and then discussion.[40]

Who needs what for induction?

Clearly all newly appointed adults who work in the school need to be welcomed into the LRC and encouraged to use it for teaching/learning and of course for their own personal reading and as a reference and study space.

Appendix 7 will help you to think about the induction needs of each group.

Different groups of adults need different information at the induction stage. Your new headteacher won't need the same information as an NQT, or the same as a new learning mentor or admin assistant.

Teaching and curriculum support staff

Teaching and support staff are prime clients if they are to develop into promoters and confident users of the LRC. Harness their support. This will help to keep your work at the heart of the curriculum and centre stage in the school. All staff, full or part time, need the VIP treatment. Their perceptions of the library and its services, and the ways in which it can support their day-to-day classroom work, are vital.

Tips for staff induction:

- Talk with your school's induction tutor to find out about induction for NQTs and other staff

- Organise the session(s) for early in the term – as part of the induction or mentoring programme. Leave it longer than this and new staff colleagues will be preoccupied with students, departments and responsibilities. They might then simply bypass the LRC and all you have to offer.

- Use small group sessions rather than working with individuals. Not only will this save time, but for the newcomers a group atmosphere will be more relaxing, will be seen as something special, and may well generate more questions and engender greater interest.

---

[40] p.23 Sir Alan Steer. *Learning Behaviour: The Report of The Practitioners' Group on School Behaviour and Discipline*. DCSF, 2005. (REF: 1950-2005DOC-EN) http://www.dcsf.gov.uk/behaviourandattendance/uploads/Learning%20Behaviour%20(published).pdf

- Provide all these potential users and supporters with:
    - some attractive leaflets about your services. These could also be be uploaded to the LRC webpages/VLE. If you're working with a big group why not have a raffle number on each leaflet (or under their seat?) and offer a prize to the lucky winner?
    - details about the exciting and useful resources that you can lend to their departments
    - information about your potential for working in partnership on curriculum topics in the LRC and and in their classrooms
    - their new library tickets/card and information about the borrowing system and library booking procedures/use of research slips etc.
    - tea/coffee and biscuits
    - a clean, tidy and attractive library to view
    - a chance to browse their own curriculum areas of the LRC and discuss their own needs with staff
    - an invitation to display work by their students
    - a library empty of other users – or at least a quiet area – interruptions can be very distracting
    - an opportunity to try out the library's ICT hardware and software
    - information about the library pages on the school's website/intranet/VLE.

Timetable the session, even if only scheduled to last for a short time. This gives it significance. Ideally, your new colleagues will have had time to think about the library and its role and will be ready to ask lots of questions. Don't expect the session to last very long. Thirty to forty-five minutes is often about right and do offer an invitation to return later.

Listen as well as provide the information that you are keen to share.

New staff, including NQTs will have had other library experiences and it is important to hear of these. Your library needs to become their library if you are to make real progress in working with these potential new users. The more they have the chance to talk to you, the more 'at home' they will feel. Remember, whatever the services and style offered in their previous school LRC, you can and will do better!

Senior leadership team newcomers

They may be feeling pleased with themselves as they have just obtained promotion and probably a rise in salary, but may also feel a little unsure of themselves in this new environment. A new headteacher, deputy and assistant head need more information too. Others will be knocking on their office door soon enough so you should be able to impress them with what the library is contributing to learning, your curriculum knowledge and the image that you're highly effective but also seeking to develop.

New Heads of Department also benefit from a bit of special treatment. You will want to be able to offer to provide the resources they need – through your own stock and through your local School Library Service. Perhaps new schemes of work will be planned or refreshed. Here is a new opportunity to work closely with a key subject area and to further build on your curriculum profile.

Remember to induct new members of the administrative staff too – invite them to have a look around, borrow your resources and tap into your information and expertise as the LRC is there as a whole school information and reading resource.

ITT (Initial Teacher Training) students also need induction too. They may not stay in your school for any length of time but they are usually enthusiastic, receptive and a fund of good ideas. It is important that they understand how they can use the LRC and this is also an opportunity to talk about links with the local school library service and its role with schools.

New Parents, Governors and the PTA

Induction is a key arm of promotion, so offer to give time to the induction of new governors, members of the school's Parent-Teacher/Friends Association and to parents of new or established students. This can bring you very good PR, much understanding and goodwill and perhaps some cash donations too.

These groups can become loyal LRC supporters if given the right introduction, and this support can be essential to developing and maintaining a successful library.

Arrange a session as part of the school's official programme. They don't have to be planned and conducted solely by LRC staff. They can be arranged as part of:

- subject based curriculum evenings
- parents' evenings
- open evenings
- the school's book week

- the PTA's Annual General Meeting
- the first governors' meeting of the new school year
- the new year staff, PTA, governors' sherry party/get together
- a library-based drive to persuade parents to donate books or money to the library
- a wider based Community event – a local literary festival, event etc.

Get them:

- browsing the books
- trying out the latest ICT equipment
- learning how to use the search facility on your library management system
- watching a short introductory in-house video
- browsing the library web pages/VLE
- trying out some of the induction activities used by the new intake groups
- being given some of the library's array of information and promotional leaflets
- looking at displays of new books and resources
- buying books displayed from the local bookshop or your School Library Service Bookshop/Exhibition Service
- taking part in a quick general knowledge quiz, making use of the LRC resources, with a small prize at the end of the evening for the winner
- listening to the LRC 's role in supporting the curriculum and then having a go at putting into order the library's/school's 'Steps to Learning' (information handling) sequence
- listening to part of a story tape created by students with the LRC as centre stage to the plot or story
- listening to a talk by a local author, illustrator, celebrity.

'Some of our governors' meetings are held in the library and when I think the opportunity is right I put out an A4 sheet with bullet points listing items that may interest them – new developments, successful projects, new resources, statistics etc. It's a nice informal way to thank them for their support.'[41]

---

[41] Claire Larson

Staff

One last thought – inducting your own staff

Many school libraries now employ at least two or more staff – perhaps job share or perhaps in manager – assistant roles. Whatever the situation it is very important to make sure that the induction given to your new colleague is as welcoming and effective as it is for all your customers.

I quote from correspondence with a lively and very effective two person library team from Droitwich Spa High School, Worcestershire.

The new Library Assistant (Jo Francis):

My initial feeling on receiving the Induction programme in the post a few days before I was due to start was a fantastic idea and how much I was looking forward to starting the job. I also felt that the school had gone to a great effort to make me feel welcome. I had a gentle but structured introduction into the school environment and all aspects of library work were covered, as well as meeting other members of staff. It was particularly enjoyable to to go on a visit to [another school] for a morning as this gave me an opportunity to see another working library.

Three months on and I'm thoroughly enjoying my job in the library and continually learning new aspects of work. My colleague… has been extremely supportive and the library is a great environment in which to work.

The Librarian (Heather Evans):

I felt that it was an extremely useful exercise for me planning the induction as it meant that… training was structured from the start; it also meant that… wasn't faced with 50+ students on Day 1 and I wasn't relying on my memory and thinking 'Have I told you about… ?'

It was good to take the time to show off our students, tour the school, visit another school, meet staff, highlight good practice and I know that… is equally enthusiastic and promoting the library.

Conclusion

Induction must be lively, memorable and above all welcoming. If you delay it, your new users may well lose interest. They will develop alternative strategies, or no strategies at all, for obtaining the information they need. They will feel intimidated by the thought of this big busy library and they will not appreciate the relevance of the library to their information and study needs.

Organising and managing induction and transition programmes takes a good deal of time and thought, in fact in a multi-staffed library it could almost be the responsibility of one full-time librarian. It is well worth the time if you can find it. Making newcomers to the school feel relaxed about coming along to the LRC to use it as part of their everyday school routine will foster positive attitudes, build your credibility and increase partnership working with students and adults across the school. Successful induction and transition programmes will provide sound foundations for both staff and students, who will be keen to return and work with you for information literacy skills sessions, reader development, Gifted and Talented programmes, summer schools and wider curriculum work. Induction and transition thinking needs constant reassessment and key dates and actions need to be put into year planners and the LRC development plan.

What ever you do for induction and however you do – make it effective, enjoyable and memorable!

Conclusion: The Induction Cycle

February onwards
Liaise with partner schools

during May and June
liaise with Year Head to learn of
- intake numbers/tutor groups
- intake abilities/Special Needs
- school liaison details – meetings, brochures etc.
- your involvement with the new Intake Day/Parents Evening

Autumn Half Term
Evaluate

The Induction Cycle for the new intake students

September/October
Carry out your Induction Programme

Plan your September induction and take an active role in the July new Intake Day and Parents' Evening

June and early July
liaise with curriculum management staff to arrange
- Sept. induction programme, staffing and timing
- curriculum use of library after the induction programme is finished

Liaise with your SLS and local library staff to find out the details of any induction schemes run by these services

Case Study 1: Broke Hall Community School

Jayne Gould

Librarian, Broke Hall Community Primary School, SLYA Honour List 2006. SLA Board member 2008 – 2011.

Induction and Transition: The Primary School Perspective

Broke Hall Community Primary School

Broke Hall is a large primary school on the eastern outskirts of Ipswich, with around 600 children on roll. There are three classes in each year group, plus the Nursery which has 52 part time places. Children join Reception in the term they become five. The school serves an area which has seen rapid expansion over the last 15 years, with much new building and families moving in.

The school itself has undergone a programme of building work, which finished in 2004. The final phase of this allowed the creation of a permanent, dedicated library area, which is open, central, and easily accessible for all children and staff.

As the librarian I work closely with all the phases of the school, on reading promotion, information literacy and ensuring the library meets all the needs of its users. We have a collection of 15,000 books, covering curriculum requirements as well as encouraging reading for pleasure. All year groups make use of the stock, choosing books to supplement classroom collections and for resources for lessons. The school subscribes to Suffolk Schools Library Service, which includes termly topic boxes for each class and a visit from the mobile library to choose extra books. In 2007, the SLS set up a support group for primary school librarians/library assistants, which meets termly. Get-togethers are hosted by a different school each time, enabling members to see a variety of libraries. The meetings feature news and updates from SLS staff, and the chance to network, exchange ideas and discuss problems with colleagues. Most of us have links with our high schools and participate in various activities with them.

Copleston High School is our catchment secondary and the one most of our pupils choose to move to from Year 6. It has 1,800 on roll, including a large Sixth Form. The school achieved specialist Sports College status in September 2001, and was graded as good with outstanding features in their most recent Ofsted inspection.

Amanda Balaam is the librarian, supported by two part time assistants. The Library at Copleston is large and well-used, with approximately 21,000 items. It is light and airy, and has been refitted in recent years, featuring modern wooden shelving, with comfortable seating as well as space to work. Years 7–11 can borrow up to three items and Years 12–13 can borrow up to six items. Most fiction books can be borrowed for two weeks. All other items can only be borrowed overnight. Students in Key Stage 3 use the Library regularly during English lessons, and a number of other subjects make use of the Library as a resource. There are a small number of computers for students to use. The Library is a popular area for the Year 7 pupils, especially during their first term at lunchtimes and after school.

Over the past few years, Amanda and I have built up a good working relationship, visiting each others schools to see the library in action and gaining an understanding of the work we both do. This enables me to prepare Broke Hall pupils for what they will encounter and for Amanda to build on the experience they have had. She has commented that she can always tell Broke Hall pupils when they use the library! Whilst partner primaries have libraries, they do not all have a librarian employed to work in the way I do with the children.

At Broke Hall, classes, including Reception, have a weekly timetabled library session, usually during reading time. These sessions are used in a variety of ways, in consultation with the teacher. I usually work with small groups, but whole classes can be accommodated if necessary. Sessions might include story times, discussion of reading choices, learning about the computerised library system or working on information literacy skills. Dewey is introduced in Year 2, so all children have a good grounding and knowledge in finding their way around the library, and in using subject index guides and other library clues. Reading promotion and extending reading choices is also an important part of what we do at Broke Hall. To encourage children to come to the library outside of class time, Years 3 to 6 have library pass cards, which allow four children from that class to come along at break or lunch time. This has proved popular, with lots of browsing and reading taking place. I also provide some paper based book related activities, such as word searches, crosswords, and bookmark templates. Children are encouraged to read a wide range of authors and genres. This is something we focus on particularly at the beginning of Year 6, getting children thinking about what they read and why they choose particular books and finding out about other books. I usually lead a whole class discussion one week, and then see smaller groups to give more individual attention. During these sessions I use a variety of games and ideas to encourage choice, for example rolling an author dice, who writes like who, giving out books in envelopes, or asking them to choose a book for a friend. Other work with Year 6 focuses on their group reading, developing their talk about books, using a range of questioning to explore their understanding of the text, express their opinions, and develop their critical thinking.

Research skills are consolidated through their work on the topics covered in history and geography in Year 6, including children's lives in Victorian times and the Second World War, and a project on coasts.

Copleston has developed a strong and successful transition programme with its feeder primaries. Early in Year 6, staff from Copleston begin a series of visits, talking to children about the school. In the Summer Term, pupils start maths and science transition tasks, with teachers coming in to introduce them. Children also begin using their Copleston literacy books and their Broke Hall reading journals are sent to the school at the end of term. During the summer holidays pupils complete a passport task.

During a two day induction visit in July, children take part in a range of activities and lessons, though numbers mean that not all of the children can do all of the lesson activities. One of these is a library session, in which the pupils complete a booklet on either a sport or a country. This involves finding set information in the resources in the Library.

Year 7 students have an induction programme lasting 5 lessons. During this they look at fiction, non-fiction and reference books, and especially focus on the Copleston Reading Champions, a reading reward programme. The Reading Champions has a list of recommended authors, some of which the Year 7 pupils will be familiar with from their reading in Year 6. This obviously helps them to feel comfortable using what is a very much larger library than they have had in their primary schools. A number of the pupils will have visited the Library before this, as it is a hive of activity during Open Night and the final of the interschool Junior Book Mastermind is held there.

Three years ago Amanda asked if we would like to take part in Junior Book Mastermind, a primary version of the competition which has been running successfully in Suffolk high schools for many years, organised by the SLS. Children in Years 7 and 8 take part in two rounds, answering questions on a book of their choice and general knowledge. Heats are held in school, the winners going forward to area finals, which decide who competes in the County Final. Several high schools have introduced the junior version, consisting of just the book round, as a transition project with their primaries. Children in Years 5 and 6 are invited to take part. Anyone interested registers with me, deciding which book they would like to use. We do try and encourage them to choose from a list that we have drawn up, as they are books Amanda has in her library and may already have questions on, but if there is a favourite they want to use, then that is fine. Amanda and her team write the questions, so if she doesn't have a particular title, then I will lend it to her. Amanda comes in to school to run the school heat, with all of Year 5 and 6 as the audience. It can be very tense and exciting, as the time limit on the round is two minutes. The top three go forward to compete at Copleston against those from partner primaries. A group of their friends and family members are invited to watch the finals. Last year Broke Hall were overall champions!

Both schools have run successful author visits, and earlier this year ran our first joint event. I was lucky enough, through my involvement with the Federation of Children's Book Groups to be offered the opportunity of a visit by popular and award winning writer Rick Riordan, author of the 'Percy Jackson' series, who was touring the UK. As the publisher asked if we could provide an audience of at least 200, I approached Amanda to see if we could use Copleston, inviting their Year 7s and Year 6 from the four feeder primaries. All the primaries accepted the invitation, and Rick spoke to a capacity audience of 600 children, entertaining and enthralling them in equal measure. Many of my pupils are now avid readers of Percy's adventures! We hope to be able to do similar events in the future, as the opportunity arises.

Whilst not strictly to do with transition, we are also developing a project where some of Copleston's pupils come into Broke Hall to read and discuss the Greenaway shortlist with younger pupils. This may include Year 9 students, or possibly those from Year 10 and 11 studying child development or Sixth Form working on language development.

In conclusion, I would say that it is vital to work closely with your partner high school, to build links and enable children to understand and make the most of their library experiences throughout their school careers.

Case Study 2: East Barnet School

Jackie Rice

School Librarian, East Barnet School, Barnet, London

Diary of Y7 Induction, September 2008

East Barnet School

I joined East Barnet School in September 2007 and was thrown headlong into Y7 Inductions for that year. East Barnet is a large mixed comprehensive school with a seven form entry, and is set in the suburbs of North London. Every Y7 class has a 'library lesson' once a week in the School Library. This is an opportunity for year seven students to learn all about the library, borrow books, spend time reading, discuss books and carry out research. The first two of these lessons are led by the Librarian as an opportunity to introduce the library to the students and for the students to borrow their first book. When I finally had a chance to draw breath, I realised that I could have done with some help with the induction programme. I registered for the SLA course, 'Crossing the Divide: Effective Induction and Transition Strategies for the Secondary School LRC' which was to take place in March 2008.

My previous post had been as Librarian in a primary school so I felt I was well qualified to know how the students felt as they arrived for their first day in their new secondary school. I also had vast experience of the types of reading which takes place in primary schools, books read, experience of primary school libraries and so on. Indeed one student from my previous school had also come to East Barnet School.

I attended the course as planned and took time afterwards to decide which of the many aspects of induction that were covered on the course to focus on. I wrote a list of items to follow up. I realised that time constrains meant that I could not cover everything. I was however very enthused about the whole idea of induction and the benefits which would be gained by giving the whole of year seven a thorough introduction to the library. I was spurred on by a belief in the benefits of ensuring that all the students are given the opportunity to read for research and pleasure and given a positive encouragement to read and appreciate the benefits of reading. I was also assisted by a very supportive and enthusiastic team of English teachers some of whom take more than one Y7 class for a library lesson each week. They also valued the chance to give every year seven student a springboard for reading which would hopefully set them on a lifetime of reading enjoyment. The school Literacy Co-ordinator has given her full support for any initiatives that I have planned.

My main aims were:

- To give a positive impression of the library
- Help the students to know who the library staff are and what the library has to offer
- Help the students to begin their reading journey.

During the summer term I made a start on the preparations.

1. My Induction talk. I based this on my talk from the previous year which had originally come from a librarian colleague. As we do not have presentation facilities in the library this was to focus on a short talk which could be given in two parts over two weeks. Week one included what the library resources are, where they are, when the library is open and an introduction to the Library Rules. Week two included further aspects of the library; how to borrow and return a book, return, renew etc. How to choose a good book, discussion of authors read in primary school and benefits of reading.

2. I designed and printed a 'Library Guide' for Y7s. This is an A5 size double page library guide which gives important library information such as staff names, library opening times, how many books can be borrowed all in very simple terms. There is also space on the front of the leaflet for the students to fill in a few personal details. One of the aims of this leaflet was to create a leaflet that will reach the students home environment – hopefully be spotted by a parent/carer and read or commented on and may be kept for future reference.

3. I prepared a Library word search – a fun activity which could be used as needed in the first two weeks.

4. I purchased more transitional level fiction books for the school library, using my knowledge of primary school reading. This included authors which students are familiar with from the primary school, especially those who have titles which would normally be found in a secondary school library such as Michael Morpurgo, Jacqueline Wilson and Roald Dahl. I also purchased some titles which would definitely be more at home in the primary school library such as Francesca Simon, Jeremy Strong and Dav Pilkey.

5. I created a 'Recommended Reading List'. I included the current year sevens in this process. The literacy co-ordinator designed a 'Book Recommendations for the New Y7' A4 sheet. This includes a table with space for the students to give their name and form and title of a recommended book and the reason it is being recommended. This is an excellent exercise in itself. We gave this out to all current year seven students to complete, collected them in and used it to put together the reading list. The reading list is an A4 triple folded leaflet and includes some of the students own comments.

6. I prepared a 'Y7 Library Reader Profile' A4 sheet. This sheet was to be given out to all students during the lesson, filled in by the students and then collected back in again. It is a chance for the library staff to get to know a little about the students' reading habits, favourite books, and previous library experience.

7   I prepared a new sign which gave the library staff names.

8   I asked around the school about the Induction Programme which we provide for year six students who have a place at East Barnet School. After much tracking down I found out the teacher responsible for this process and had a chat with her. It was too late to be included in this years Y6 visit but hopefully I had sown a seed for next year.

9   I designated one lunch time a week as 'Y7s only' in the school library.

September 2008 soon came around. The new Y7 classes would soon begin. I made it a priority to ensure that I had all the new year seven details correctly input on the library management software and I made a file of class lists so that I would be able to familiarise myself with their names before the lessons.

I checked the printing was all up to date of the various leaflets – 200 copies of everything that needed to be distributed. We ensured the fiction area of the library had plenty of the newly processed transition books on display.

I prepared a memo for the Y7 library lessons English teachers to explain how the first two library lessons would work. The actual inductions were like a military operation. I kept a note of which class inductions were completed and which leaflets had been distributed. The national 'Booked Up' initiative coincided with the beginning of the new school year so we were able to get on board with this and ensure each year seven student received their free book via the school library. This also created a lot of enthusiasm and a real buzz throughout the year group, especially when the new books arrived.

The Reader Profile provided some very interesting information which can be used in all aspects of library planning. For example we found out that apart from speaking/reading English at home students in Y7 also speak/read thirteen other languages including Hebrew, Polish, Greek and French. The students have come from a total of seventeen different primary schools. 35% came from the first main feeder school, 13% from the next feeder school and twelve students were the only one from their primary school to come to East Barnet School. An amazing 20 students answered that they had been a library helper in their previous schools. 62% of the students answered that they were members of their public library. Some of the authors the students mentioned as their favourite author were Anthony Horowitz, J. K. Rowling, Terry Pratchett, Darren Shan, Terry Deary, Malorie Blackman, Stephanie Meyer and Lemony Snicket. Some of the reasons given by students as to why they thought they might like to use their school library were: 'because you can see as soon as you come in the fantastic books', 'because I love reading', 'because it's like being an adult working late on the computer', 'because it has newspapers', 'because there are more books than my primary school'. This information gave us an amazing insight into the students' interests, reading habits and backgrounds.

Over the last six months since the Induction, the classes still come to the library for their library lessons. Many pupils have become great readers and relish this opportunity to spend time reading and learning research skills. As a continuation of the process we will offer the Y7s the opportunity to take part in a Lit. Quiz organised by school librarians within the Borough of Barnet, and we will also be taking book recommendations from the current Forms with a view to producing another reading list. At the beginning of the summer term we have an author visit planned for the whole year group to take part in. This term I also hope to find the time to visit our main feeder schools; meet the current Y6 students and visit their library and hopefully meet their teacher/librarian if they have one. I have kept some copies of suitable books to take as a gift for their school library.

I will be returning to chat with the Head of Lower School responsible for Induction and hopefully including a 'Reading Suggestions' leaflet in the pack which goes home to Y6 students. We also continue to try to raise the profile of the library at the school Y6 Transition Open Evening held in the Autumn Term each year – when students and their parents visit the school for the first time. We are planning a library programme for this evening and leaflets geared to new parents.

Overall the process seemed to me to be very successful. Towards the end of their Y7 I would like to ask the students for their suggestions as to how they felt library induction went and update the process accordingly. One aspect which we need to find time to make more of next year is the Reader Profiles. We did look at these but did not have time to compile a results chart for each form which would have been really helpful. During the year we also produced a booklet-style Reading Passport which we intended to give to each student to encourage reading. By the time the booklet was produced the main impetus for giving it out had passed, but we will definitely use this next year. I am very satisfied about how the process went.

I felt we really made every effort to achieve our goals and I do think that this year we will have achieved them.

Thanks also to my library colleagues, past and present at East Barnet School.

Case Study 3: Werneth School

Nikki Heath

Librarian, Werneth School, Stockport and SLA School Librarian of the Year 2008

Werneth Wonders – Library Induction for the New Intake Students

Werneth School, Stockport

Induction is always a very important time for students who are beginning secondary school. The focus for their five years there will be on consistently producing quality work and research in order to achieve good results. These results will allow them to access their chosen career. It is therefore essential that students are introduced to the library and its resources as soon as possible. They need to be aware from the minute that they step through the doors that not only can regular reading improve GCSE results, but that the library can help them to achieve in other ways, too.

Induction in some ways is a two way street; it is our way of encouraging the students to familiarise themselves with where the resources are and how they can use them, but also an opportunity for us to begin to become familiar with the students and their reading and research habits. In some schools, this is the only opportunity that librarians will have to meet every new student. Thankfully at Werneth I am fortunate enough to see all year sevens, eights and nines once a fortnight.

By the time students arrive for their official first day at Werneth, the majority are already familiar with the school and its library, for they have had the opportunity to visit the school at least three times. In 2008, I also went into the public libraries and met many of them as part of the 'Book Idol' scheme. I also visited schools with the librarian in charge of Bredbury library where possible to promote the Summer Reading Scheme, Team Read.

I decided early on that it was important for new students to be relaxed and comfortable using the library, and for it to be viewed as a non-threatening, friendly, welcoming environment. Therefore the activities in place for all visits to school had been designed with fun and incentives in mind, but with an underlying information literacy focus.

On Open Evening, which takes place in the October of their year six year, the parents and students take part in a 'quick quiz' whilst on a learning journey through the school and enter a Prize Draw. On Fun Day, which takes place on a Saturday in June, the library runs a 'murder mystery' activity. Students examine our 'Miss Teree' crime scene and then work in small groups to solve the crime. During this task, students allocate a scribe, and cannot pass clues to each other. This means they have to read their clues and work as a team, allowing them to get to know other students. When they arrive in July for their 'taster day', students answer a questionnaire about their reading habits and we play 'The Reading Game'. During the genre changes, we ask students to move around in the most inventive way possible, to keep them active, add some fun and to keep their brains working! The questionnaires are taken away and a report about the new intake's attitudes to reading and overall reading habits is compiled and made available to all staff the following week.

During the last half of the summer term, Stockport Libraries run 'Book Idol'. This is a one off, fun activity which is offered to all year sixes in the region. Students work in groups, examining their chosen 'shiny bag' book, and promote it using the cover, blurb and opening chapter. All students then vote for their favourite book, which is taken back to school for them to read. All Stockport librarians were invited to get involved and I jumped at the chance to work in partnership with the schools and the librarians to support the task. The students again got to know me a little better, and I was able to talk to them about their current reading habits, too. With Anna, the Librarian in Charge, I also went into schools to promote the Summer reading scheme, which again introduces the library motto of 'Reading reaps rewards' and that it can be fun, too!

When our intake finally arrive in September, they spend just over 2 days in our 'Werneth Cares' induction program. During this time, the whole year group rotates around the senior leadership team, learning about the school. They discover what type of learner they are, are introduced to the idea of taking responsibility for their own learning, values, hydration, and visit the library. Here, they take the NFER reading test with a member of SLT and then work with me for half an hour.

Rather than being talked at, I feel it is important that the students get to explore for themselves. For 20 minutes they are allowed to look around, and with the 'new books' stand bursting with recent acquisitions, students are told that they are allowed to borrow and the procedure for doing so. I also tell them where the fiction and fact books are, and that if they can't find what they are looking for to come to me for help. It is fabulous to watch this lesson, as many have not stepped into a library environment over the Summer and this is the first opportunity they have had to browse, read up to date magazines on their favourite pastimes and interests, borrow books and generally soak up a library atmosphere. I always compare this lesson to letting a 5 year old loose in a sweet shop; most don't know where to go first! There will be plenty of time to go into detail and teach them how to use the library properly, and as long as they know the basics they can borrow books from day one. The sooner they get into the routine of taking books out once a fortnight, the more chance I have of them enjoying the resources we have and turning them into 'regulars' at break and lunchtimes, too. At the end of this first lesson, students are given a 'reading race' booklet, which encourages them to read different genres of books for reward points. We have a thermometer chart on the wall for them to recommend the books they have read during their first term of the Reading Race, with each thermometer being worth a reward point. It is a great way of encouraging peer recommendation, as well as giving them somewhere to celebrate and share with others the books that they have read.

Once the 'Werneth Cares' program finishes, students begin their regular timetable. Within this, they will visit the library once a fortnight for a series of information literacy lessons. The first five of these can be loosely classed as induction sessions as they ensure that students know exactly where the different areas of the library are, and teach them to use Searchstar, the library catalogue. I changed my first 'whole' induction lesson this year and, instead of handing out a 'rules' leaflet and talking them through it, which I was beginning to find tedious, used the Cephalonian induction method instead. This consists of using an interactive PowerPoint, using a series of coloured slides containing questions and answers about the basic library procedures. The students are randomly given cards as they come into the library and pair up with the person sitting next to them. As the cards show up on the PowerPoint, the student with the corresponding card reads the question out, and their partner reads the answer, which is on the display. I found that the students stay engaged during this as they are looking out for their question, and there are a few video snippets in there which have them laughing and keep them interested, too. After a 'quick question' session, where I answer any other queries which the students might have, the 'quiz quiz trade' plenary re-enforces the rules learned during the lesson. There is time left to issue and return books.

In 2008 this was followed up with a 'Team Read' session, where students look at what they have read over the holidays and then this will be tied in to the 2009 Summer Reading Challenge, and the activities for this lesson will be downloaded from the 'Their Reading Futures' website, provided by The Reading Agency. All types of reading, including magazines and text messages, online chat and books are included in this, and students add up their 'reading points' and set a reading target for the next lesson. We then produce a graph and pie chart showing what everyone in the group has read. Students who have still not registered their finger do so, and they are then sent around the fiction shelves, looking for particular authors within the fiction genres. This is a race activity, with students being put into teams, and the team with the most answers receiving rewards points. It is a 'sneaky' way of teaching the students how the fiction books are arranged, and again re-enforces that the library can be fun, as well as being a place where they can earn reward points. A sleep and learning lesson follows, and students are asked to fill out a sleep diary for two weeks, and are asked to read for ten minutes every night before going to bed. Many students ask if they can continue to do this, and some have said that the diary has helped them to identify the best way for them to relax before going to sleep.

Two 'Orientation Day' lessons are then taught. The first, partly written by Janet Clarke, the previous librarian, asks students to find general areas of the library, with a few 'trick' questions thrown in to keep them on their toes. They then design their ideal library of the future, which they are told they can present to the rest of the class, if they wish. The second 'Orientation Day' lesson asks them to find specific resources within the fiction, non-fiction, reference, magazine, newspaper and PC areas, again ensuring that each individual student has looked around every part of the library and understands where the resources are kept. This begins to introduce independent learning, ensuring that they can find resources for themselves. To see what the students have remembered from their Cephalonian Induction, which by now is around eight weeks ago, we include a quick quiz here and a copy of the rules for them to refer to if they are unsure, with reward points offered to those who get every question correct. A final lesson has students working in pairs, competing to find books on the shelves versus using the library catalogue. Vague questions such as 'A book by Tony Robinson' have been deliberately included to illustrate how important it is to use the library catalogue when searching for resources, and showing how much time this can save them. They also learn how to access websites from Searchstar, too. Using the catalogue to manage their loans and reservations is also explained during this lesson.

Library induction at Werneth begins 'for real' in September, and can take until mid January. Although it would be great to have a solid, three hour session to quickly run through these lessons, I feel this would be too much information for many of them to take in at once, and activities wherever possible are already broken up into ten or twenty minute chunks to keep the students focussed and on task. It is, therefore, a slow process, with lesson starters where possible touching upon what has been previously taught. The same sessions are delivered to all abilities, with the difference being in the 'chunking' of the tasks. These induction sessions give all students the basic building blocks necessary to be able to use any library wherever they might be, and this foundation is then built upon during the information literacy lessons.

Case Study 4: Southwark Book Award

Laura Taylor

Librarian, City of London Academy (Southwark)

www.southwarkbookaward.org.uk

Southwark Schools' Book Award: A reading/transition/ICT project

The setting up of the Southwark Schools' Book Award was the result of several ideas coinciding. Having given a presentation at an lea transition conference, where I had been asked to highlight some ways in which the school library could support transition, the borough's secondary English consultant was keen to further discuss ways in which we might work together. At the same time I had contacted some local primaries, keen to visit and find out what their libraries were like to inform myself of their students' library experience, so as to tailor my own Y7 library inductions, and also to invite some of their students to visit our library. Having previously worked in the borough's Schools' Library Service I was already familiar with many of the local primaries. Working in one of the recently set up brand new Academies however few of these local links or contacts between schools had been made, and at that stage we did not have a teacher in charge of transition. I was also considering setting up some kind of book group in my new school, on a similar model to the recently discontinued Askews' 'Torchlight Award' which we had shadowed with local primary schools in my previous Lambeth school as part of the Norwood Achievement Partnership (NAP).

I felt it was important to inform myself also of the new Y7 students' reading choices so I had used a number of strategies: obtaining details of their Reading Ages from our Literacy teacher; using an idea picked up from an earlier edition of this SLA guideline and sending postcards to each of their primary schools asking them to let me know their favourite books/authors; familiarising myself with the KS2 Literacy strategy and its themes; and carrying out reading interviews with them when they joined secondary school. Meeting with the English advisor however it became clear that the existing KS2/3 English transition units were not consistently used in all feeder primary schools and portfolios of evidence of KS2 work produced were not always forthcoming from some Y6 teachers.

Keen to set up some kind of book group where students could read, discuss, write on-line reviews, blog and vote on their favourite books I considered the possible options. Most of the existing book awards – Carnegie, Costa, Guardian, etc. – took no account of students' preferences and whilst recent Carnegie shortlists had undoubtedly included sophisticated texts of great literary merit, there had been lengthy debate about the suitability of some of the titles for younger secondary school students. Those awards that did involve students in the voting – The Red House and Blue Peter Awards – had no online reviewing facility or blog and I felt incorporating ICT into any reading project would be an added incentive for many of our students. Several local authorities – usually the public and/or Schools' Library Services – had already set up their own local awards so clearly a precedent had been set in other LEAs. Most of these however were limited to secondary schools or secondary age pupils.

So setting up a pilot project combining these elements – focusing on Y6 and Y7's reading choices, transition and a book award linking our school with local feeder primaries – seemed the ideal solution. One other local secondary school expressed an interest in also getting involved in this first pilot year.

We were advised and encouraged at this initial stage by the excellent Lyn Hopson of Don Valley School, who had been involved in setting up a similar scheme for Doncaster schools. She was able to give us the benefit of her experience, point out any pitfalls, as well as recommending the SLA's own web designer, Nigel Smith of Intexta, and also a drama consultant, Dave Cryer.

Our first meetings were a valuable development in themselves as this was for many primary teachers the first time they had been invited in to a local secondary school and certainly their first visit to their new local Academy. For the secondary English teachers involved this was for many the first time they had met with their primary counterparts, and for local public library staff this was often the first contact they had had with the borough's secondary schools. We were fortunate in having the support of our LEA secondary English consultant who was able to secure some transition funding for us. This meant we could supply every participating school with multiple copies of the six shortlisted titles – usually four or five copies of each book per class. Primary colleagues recommended that the best timing for the project would be the Summer Term as a post Key Stage 2 SATS activity. The public libraries agreed to support the award with displays of the books in all branches and the involvement of their Chatterbook groups.

At these initial meetings in the Autumn Term all schools are encouraged to suggest and bring along likely titles. Our book suppliers provide us with a range of recent titles that meet our specifications (significant titles published in the UK in the last year which would appeal to Y6/7) on a sale or return basis, so along with copies of books from the local public libraries and our own schools we are able to spend two to three months sifting from approximately 50 titles down to our shortlist of six. Some schools take the opportunity to trial possible titles with their students and so involve them in the process at an early stage. We are keen to ensure students of all reading abilities and tastes are involved in the award so ensure we select a range of genres that will be of broad appeal, are accessible to as many students as possible but will also we feel be popular reads of some literary merit, possibly introducing students to new authors. We then as a group share responsibility for contacting publishers for publicity and possible prizes, producing schemes of work based on the books, designing review booklets, posters, and bookmarks, or writing playscripts, quiz questions and slideshow presentations to introduce the award and the books.

A key element in this transition link are the visits made by each secondary school librarian to their feeder primaries. Early in the Summer Term the librarian, often accompanied by a teacher in charge of transition, visits the Y6 classes with a group of ex-students from that primary school to both introduce the award, the website and the shortlisted books but also to answer questions about moving to 'big school'. This link between schools develops further throughout each year's award, with joint events held in each secondary school involving Year 6 and 7 students in drama or creative writing workshops focusing on the books.

In our first year we set up a blog but were able to fund a much more interactive website in the second year. We included on this a number of quizzes, on-line games created using the what2learn (www.what2learn.com) and classtools (www.classtools.net) websites, suggestions for activities about the books, play scripts based on some of the texts, and the facility for students to record podcasts using the free Voicethread website (www.voicethread.com). In our second year we received nearly 1,000 reviews/comments – all of which had to be moderated – a major consideration when setting up the website. Returning home after a day's work to 100 posts all needing to be checked for any 'inappropriate' comments is a mammoth task and best shared between group organisers if possible. In practice there have only been a couple of instances of such 'silliness' and class teachers stress the importance of responsible ICT use.

Rather than have one large final event, where inevitably numbers who could attend would have to be limited, we decided to continue the emphasis on local 'families of schools' by holding a number of individual celebratory final events hosted in each secondary school towards the end of the Summer Term, where every participating student attends. This is very much the grand finale of the whole process – having 300 Year 6 and 7 students in our school hall all cheering and shouting for their favourite book is a sight (and sound!) to behold. I feel a little like a game show host as teams from each school compete in a 'Who wants to be a millionaire' style quiz on the books, read book reviews or give presentations. Some schools invite one of the shortlisted authors, who gives a short talk and sign copies of their books, or a storyteller. The excitement is palpable as everyone waits to hear the result of the vote and the name of the winning book. Prizes and certificates are awarded for best reviews on the website, keenest readers who have managed to read all six books and winning teams from each school. We were fortunate in our second year to secure the wonderful prize of a pod on the London Eye – 25 free seats – allowing us to select one student from each school as a winner. Appropriately – and quite coincidentally – our winning book that year was in fact Siobhan Dowd's *The London Eye Mystery*! The publishers supplied a magnificent cake and goody bags, and we were delighted when local MP Simon Hughes met us all at 'The Eye' for a photo-shoot and to congratulate the winners.

We are now entering our third year and have extended the project from the initial two secondaries and their seven feeder primaries, to seven secondaries and their feeder primaries – a total of 25 schools plus the local public libraries Chatterbook groups. We estimate 1,000 students across the borough will be involved this year. We are keen to involve parents and possibly more departments in our schools so it becomes more of a cross curricular project involving English, drama, and art departments working with the library. Some art departments will be working with students on producing alternative book covers, and drama teachers and consultants, will be running workshops bringing the books to life.

We survey all staff and students each year so as to refine and improve the whole project. This has led to our starting the project a little earlier than initially planned so as to give as many students as possible an opportunity to read all six books. Feedback has been universally positive with comments from teachers such as 'I thought it was perfect!'; 'pupils reading speed and enthusiasm increases with children outdoing each other'; 'good range of books especially for the boys'; and from children, 'the books that were picked were a great choice'; 'I would never really have read six books in a couple of weeks if it wasn't for the book award'; 'because of the Southwark Book Award we did lots of cool things'; 'it has inspired me to read more books in the future'; 'the games are cool'; 'I will enjoy reading at secondary school'.

Funding has been secured from the LEA for another year at least but we may have to look elsewhere in future or encourage schools to buy their own copies of the books.

The knock-on effects have been the biggest bonus. The participating Y6 classrooms are now resourced with sets of each of the succeeding year's award's shortlisted titles meaning new Y7s increasingly share common reading experiences, which is a boon for myself and their English teachers. In my own school we are linked with just three feeder primaries (six classes) but over a third of our 180 intake had taken part in the Book Award, many via links made with the other secondaries involved.

Most important though has been the developing relationships between schools, the links made between the LEA, schools and public libraries, and of course the familiarity new Y7s now have with their 'big' school and their librarian.

Why the Book Award?

- lack of information about Y6 students' reading experiences
- evidence of students' academic regression by the end of Y7
- to build relationships between key partners
- to empower students by giving them a voice and a vote as to their reading choices
- encourage reading for pleasure

Key partners

- LEA advisory staff
- Secondary school librarians
- Y6 class teachers
- Primary/secondary literacy co-ordinators
- Y7 English teachers
- Heads of transition/Head of Y7
- Local public library staff
- Book suppliers
- Web designer/ICT technicians
- Drama teachers/consultants

The Books

- Six titles – a range of genres, levels, gender appeal, with due regard for equal opportunities
- published in last 12 months and preferably available in paperback (to save on costs)

References

The Impact of school transitions and transfers on pupil progress and attainment. (Galton, Gray and Ruddock, 1999)

http://www.southwarkbookaward.org.uk

http://www.slideshare.net/LTay007

http://uk.youtube.com/watch?v=opaOmrEoWFM

Case Study 5: Pembroke School

Liz Smith

Librarian, Pembroke School, Pembrokeshire

SLA Board member 2008 – 2011 Chair of the SLA Training Group

Love at first sight – first impressions mean so much! – Year 6 Induction

Pembroke School, Pembrokeshire

This case study is intended to outline just one of the many exciting and innovative transition schemes which exist to bridge the gap between primary and secondary school, and aims to show the planning, organisation, considerations and potential problems, as well as the numerous benefits, of one particular scheme in Pembroke School in West Wales, an 11–18 mixed comprehensive with 1,500+ students.

Starting at a large, geographically extensive comprehensive school can be a daunting experience for anyone, let alone a new pupil leaving the relative security of their primary school. The potential for the Library to play a vital role in smoothing this transition is considerable – a welcoming place and a friendly face to rely on when everything seems so strange.

Although the forging of strong primary-secondary links is now becoming commonplace, at the time our scheme started ten years ago, we were one of the first individual departments in our school to develop a programme of visits, independent of the established 'Welcome Day'. Together with my line manager, who was in charge of the whole transition process, I proposed a series of visits to our Library by Year 6 pupils from our eleven partner primary schools, an intake of about 250 to 325 pupils each year. These visits have gone from strength to strength, each year aiming to build on and improve the last, forming an acknowledged and essential part of the school calendar for both our school and all its feeder schools.

Planning

Headteachers of all our partner primary schools were fully supportive when a proposal for the scheme was raised at our 'Family of Schools' meeting. Led by my line manager, full backing by our School Management Team was instrumental in getting the visits established and ensuring their continuation. It was decided that visits should take place in June/July after KS2 SATs had finished. Although this is now no longer such an issue since SATs have been abolished in Wales, we have kept to this timing. The number of visits per school is dependent on the numbers of pupils – our larger partner schools require two or three visits to accommodate all pupils. A timetable is circulated of available slots, and schools contact me to book a mutually convenient time.

In preparing the sessions I compiled an induction booklet, including quizzes and activities designed to familiarise pupils with the Library and its stock and services. Despite very positive feedback after the first year, I felt it necessary to re-evaluate the sessions in conjunction with primary staff to ensure that they were as effective as possible and that skills developed in primary school were being built on and extended at Pembroke. I therefore arranged to meet two teachers representing the Family of Schools to discuss pupils' prior experience of libraries, and to consider skills and activities we might include. Since then, the sessions have been evaluated each year and modifications made to the programme and induction booklet according to need. Prior to the sessions each year, I consult our SMT primary-secondary liaison representative and our Special Educational Needs Coordinator to maximise my knowledge of pupils so that I am aware of and therefore able to respond to individual needs.

Primary colleagues agreed to do some work to prepare pupils for their visit; materials are sent out for this purpose, including an activity for pupils to design their ideal school library. Not only does this produce some ready-made display material, it also provides some invaluable insights into pupils' expectations of, and suggestions for, their new school library!

Content

Making our new school members feel at home in the Library from the outset, and demonstrating the vital role it can play for each of them during their time at Pembroke, has always been fundamental to our approach. A bright, colourful badge helps to introduce me to the pupils; they are asked to reciprocate using sticky badges so that I can address each by name.

Only too aware that first impressions are paramount, I endeavour to ensure that the Library is looking its best, and that relevant stock is prominently displayed to grab pupils' attention and make them desperate to return. It is an ideal opportunity to promote our reading clubs, authors familiar and new, and popular topics of interest. Although it is not possible at this stage for pupils to be entered on our library management system, I keep aside any items they would like to borrow for collection in the first week of the new school year. Not only does this immediately establish them as borrowers at this stage, it also means that they will come back in the first week. Most do, and a personal reminder sent via their new form tutor reminds those who have forgotten.

I was anxious that the induction booklet should provide a structure for the morning sessions, but also that the activities themselves should emphasise the enjoyment libraries can bring and that they should develop learning skills in a fun way. The aims of the session are shared with the pupils on the cover of their booklets. The activities planned take account of many learning styles, incorporating elements for visual, auditory and kinaesthetic learners and focusing on teamwork and paired work as well as on individual tasks. In recent years, I have incorporated a quick starter activity to get pupils thinking. On the flipchart or electronic whiteboard, I elicit from pupils the six things they expect from their new school library; things to borrow or use, or things they expect their library to do. When we first started the visits, I used a blank map of the Library which pupils seemed to enjoy completing as they found their way around and discovered what we had to offer. After a couple of years, however, I increasingly felt that the activity was perhaps more about map-reading and less about encouraging pupils to handle and interact with the resources we are all keen to enthuse them with on their first visit! In its place, I now include a simple but popular and effective activity which involves pupils exploring the Library in small teams. Each team is given a pack of colour-coded cards (matching the Library's signguiding), each with a particular area on it and any relevant spine labels to look out for. Every team has a card for the Fiction and for the Information Books; cards with other sections (such as Puzzle and Quiz Books, Poetry, Graphic Novels, DVDs, Magazines, Bitesize Reads, Jokebooks, etc) are distributed across the teams to keep things fresh. Every pupil finds and explores the Fiction and Information Books, plus a choice of any two other sections from their team's cards, and chooses one item of stock from each area which appeals to them. They are encouraged to keep hold of these items and log them down in their booklets, together with a brief reason for choosing them. After a specified time, we return to our places with our choices and each group shares their choices with the others and outlines their reasons for choosing them. This has proved an ideal opportunity to look at how we set about choosing, to investigate other titles/authors pupils might like, and to read juicy extracts to tempt them.

Following on from this activity, an individual quiz enables pupils to discover information about using the Library from the Library website,[42] and from signs in the Library. One quiz question asks pupils to go to the 'Reading Zone' area of the website and post a note of what they would like to borrow in September. We hope that this will make them feel part of the school already and promote use of the website as well. Using a card-sort activity, pupils are also introduced briefly to the school's 'Helping Hand' information literacy model.[43] Sneaky preparation for their work in Year 7!

As well as being introduced to the Library as a place of learning and fun, pupils are familiarised with its code of conduct. Having learned that food and drink are not acceptable in the Library, they also discover that permitted exceptions also apply! Food and drink are a key element of reading club meetings and events, including Year 6 visits. Needless to say, this is well received!

Plentiful giveaways such as bookmarks, stickers and an induction certificate are a popular and perfect round-off to a lively, constructive and very positive morning!

---

[42] http://www.pembroke.school-library.co.uk/
[43] a modified version of the 'Hand-Up' model developed by Lucy Pearson when she was at John Cabot Academy, Bristol.

Continuity

Primary staff are encouraged to take pupils' induction booklets back to school with them in order to complete two follow-up activities at a time convenient to them before the end of term. Pupils make comments, drawings and doodles reflecting their first impressions of their new school library, as well as completing a library and reading profile – both activities make for highly informative, sometimes amusing, touching, and at times eye-opening reading. Once this invaluable feedback has been read and points for action for the coming year and next year's visits noted, pupils' own booklets are then made available to them for use in their first year.

One year we tried to bridge the Summer holiday gap with a bookmark competition, issuing pupils with a bookmark template to design, including details of their Summer holiday reads; the six week gap seemed to prove too long to sustain this, and we began looking for other ideas which might work better. We have had some success with a postcard promotion, where pupils leave their visit with a blank postcard which they send to their new form tutor telling them about their favourite reads, what they're currently reading and their interests. This has proven more sustainable if run in conjunction with primary colleagues and parents. The postcards are then raffled and prizes awarded in the first weeks of September. The postcards also then form an eye-catching reading display in pupils' new tutor rooms.

Considerations

A number of considerations must be addressed in running a scheme such as this. Given the numbers involved in our case, the Library must be closed for at least fourteen sessions (practically three lessons out of five each day the visits take place). Every effort is made to minimise disruption, with advance notice of the visits and increased publicity for the resource box facility (boxes of resources bookable for classroom use available on short-term loan), and offers to support all staff as far as possible. Despite the inevitable inconvenience to staff and pupils, I have found colleagues to be extremely supportive, acknowledging the value of the visits. It is also admittedly a huge time commitment for me in leading fourteen sessions, but one which I feel reaps many immediate and long-term benefits.

Fortunately, a number of our schools are relatively near, and thanks to the commitment of primary schools to the scheme, most transport issues are overcome by minibus and with parental assistance in the case of the smaller schools. Money has so far been made available through 'Family of Schools' funding to cover transport costs.

Benefits

The benefits of such a scheme are both invigorating and far-reaching:

- Scheduling the visits in advance of the new school year highlights the session and lifts it above the hectic first weeks of term. Pupils have already had an insight into what the Library can do for them, as well as what it expects of them, and are keen to re-visit as soon as possible.

- The high profile of the visits further establishes the Library's central role in teaching and learning within the school – and beyond – with primary colleagues and parents.

- Working closely with the pupils for a morning enables me to begin to get to know them and gives me a head start in learning their names and discovering their individual needs and reading preferences. This personal knowledge can make an immediate and valued difference for pupils.

- Parents are alerted from the outset to the part the Library can play in their child's development and education. Pupils at the new intake Parents' Evening bring their parents in to show them the Library and enthuse about what they did on their visit, keen to demonstrate their knowledge. Comments made by parents include: 'She's been talking about her visit at home ever since!' and 'I think you'll be seeing a lot of him in the Library!'

Every year as the programme of visits reaches its end, although exhausted, I feel exhilarated by the pupils' sheer enthusiasm, wanting to bottle it and sprinkle it liberally! The scheme has demonstrated its far-reaching impact already; the scope for extending this is limitless.

Case Study 6: Cheadle Hulme High School

Claire Larson

Previously library manager, Cheadle Hulme High School, Stockport. An 11–16 comprehensive with Language College status. 1350+ students.

Don't forget the adults! – giving new staff a cool LRC welcome

Cheadle Hulme High School, Stockport

This case study was written in 2005 and records library and school policy at the time.

Introduction

LRC induction for new staff usually takes place at the beginning of the school year and is part of the general staff induction. It is one element of a rolling programme that includes sessions on the curriculum, pastoral issues, student tracking and school administration. This greatly benefits me as it is broadcasting the message that the LRC is part of the integral business of the school and that the Leadership Group are prepared to invest time and effort in ensuring new staff can find out all that it has to offer.

Why Do It?

From my point of view the advantages of running a staff induction session seem to be threefold.

- Firstly it is a chance for me to meet new staff and introduce myself. In a sprawling secondary school with over a hundred staff this is extremely valuable.

- Secondly, it is an opportunity for the staff to find their way to the LRC and see what it has to offer.

- Thirdly and perhaps most importantly it's my chance to take things a step further and shape opinions; this is the one occasion when I have a captive audience and I am keen to raise their expectations of what the LRC has to offer.

Who Attends?

All new staff are invited to the induction session, so I am likely to have an eclectic group including heads of department, newly qualified teachers, classroom support assistants, and with workforce reform, members of staff closely involved in working with pupils but who are not actually teachers. It is also possible that every curriculum area could be represented, or just a few.

On The Day

The session takes place after school and the LRC is closed to students. On one occasion I did involve the student librarians in preparing for and helping during the session. It was not a success as my volunteer helpers were excessively exuberant and the staff excessively withdrawn, not an ideal combination. I soon realised that by the end of a busy day the staff are tired and deserve some time to themselves. Likewise, I want to concentrate on the staff without having to consider the pupils' needs as well. All round this occasion seems to work better without the pupils present.

I usually put out examples of projects for people to peruse and get a feel for how the LRC is used. These are out on display alongside the most important resources of all – the coffee jar and the biscuit tin. The nature of schools means that people arrive in dribs and drabs and starting with a coffee gives people a few minutes to collect themselves and there is something for them to look at while we are waiting for everyone to arrive.

How Long Is The Session?

Attending courses and conferences has taught me that we always appreciate something when we can see the benefit, so when planning the session I try to see it from the staff's point of view: 'What's in it for me?' This is certainly important for harassed, pressured teachers who seem to be drowning under a mountain of paperwork demanding levels, targets and next year's development plan, and who might be going home to prepare tomorrow's lessons, tonight's tea and their daughter's birthday party. Work-life balance is currently the buzz phrase so I try to keep it interesting, relevant and short, packing plenty into a thirty-minute session.

When planning the session I always keep in mind the following:

- Be positive
- Use the time well.
- Present the basics in a leaflet
- Remember: 'What's in it for me?'
- Make it memorable
- Speak generally but use examples
- Follow it up.

Be Positive

New staff, visiting the LRC for the first time do not want to be greeted with grumbles from me about miniscule budgets and the impossibility of supporting a hundred unexpected requests for information on microbes with four books and a few computers. We are all aware of the problems of running a frantically busy library service on a budgetary shoestring. Fortunately LRC Managers are renowned for their creative flair, hard work and large dollops of humour and I see this as the perfect opportunity to try and exercise all of the above! I've realised it helps to put on a performance and act like a virtual cheerleader; waving my pom-poms in praise of our fantastic LRC and all that it has to offer.

Use the Time Well

Time is of the essence. In half an hour I can't hope to touch on everything the LRC offers. The aim is to give a taste of the areas I think the staff would find most useful and to present it in such a way that they will remember it and come back for more.

Present the basics in a leaflet

Talking about issue figures and how many books you can borrow is worthy but dull, so I usually present such basics in a leaflet. These days everyone is conscious of marketing and presentation and I enlisted help from the Graphics Department when producing my introductory leaflet. They came up with a greetings card style brochure that is eye-catching and can stand up on a desk or be pinned to a notice board and (hopefully) referred to again. Just to draw peoples' attention to the content I usually mention one or two points while the coffee is being poured and hope that they will peruse it for themselves later on.

What's in it for me?

Continuing the premise that we respond favourably when we can see what's in it for us, I try to do a bit of homework beforehand about the people attending. I am likely to be meeting staff at all stages of their careers and from all subject areas, so I like to find out whether there are many newly qualified teachers and which curriculum areas will be represented. I also check if there are likely to be heads of department or people with particular interests such as numeracy, literacy, the special needs or pastoral care. All the information helps me to decide which examples I will use during the session.

I also keep in mind that their previous experience of libraries will be varied. Some will have come from schools where the LRC is a fantastic support to the curriculum, while others may have worked in schools where this is just at the embryonic stage. Some will have no experience of using the LRC to support their teaching at all while others will be way ahead of us.

Make it Memorable

It is well recorded that youngsters have a concentration span in minutes roughly equivalent to their age, but it doesn't follow that if a sixteen year old can concentrate for 16 minutes a forty year old can concentrate for 40 minutes. After a busy day at work it's likely to be considerably less. I learnt from a public speaking course that to make it memorable you should aim to concentrate on three things that you want people to take away with them and remember. To reinforce the significance of these I often write three headings on the flip chart.

The pointers I usually choose are as follows:

- That the LRC is a useful whole school resource – I emphasise that information-handling skills are taught through the curriculum and I also mention that our most successful projects generally start in the classroom, continue in the LRC and return to the classroom for completion.

- That an invisible chord does not tie me to the LRC. I'm ready and willing to visit classes to talk about specific resources, introduce research skills or whatever is appropriate.

- Finally to give a feel for what the LRC is really about – the students, I mention some of the special projects and how the Resources Centre is used during social times.

(One lesson I took away for the future was a plan to use a PowerPoint presentation to reinforce the above points. I had watched our Head Teacher selling the school to prospective Y7s with one and it was extremely powerful, especially being interspersed with images of all the activities going on in school. I intend to to arm myself with a digital camera from now on!)

Talk generally but give specific examples

The above three points can be made most successfully in the context of the people attending, so if the new head of History is one of the delegates I will probably refer to the Year 7 History project on Ancient China which concentrates on using a variety of resources and reading for information.

If some of the delegates are NQTs I might talk about how the LRC can be booked for project work and how I am keen to be involved in planning and developing projects.

To give everyone a feel for the LRC during social times I will probably mention the chess club and the reading club, the work done by the student librarians, the book fair, poetry lunch times and the puzzle challenge day.

To emphasise the value of the LRC as a whole school resource I will mention that the catalogue is networked and can be accessed from any computer in the school. I will make sure that I show them how to access it too. I might also mention projects that have benefited from resources obtained elsewhere such as the Schools Library Service.

The examples I give during the session change from year to year, depending on who attends, new developments in LRC services and which areas of the LRC services are particularly in demand at that moment.

Finally I invite questions and comments and suggest that people might wish to stay to view some of the software, or look through the examples of projects up on display. Not everyone will stay and I don't take that personally, (work-life balance again!) but there are usually one or two who might have queries or even want to discuss possibilities for projects.

Follow it Up

I suppose the most important aspect of induction is to follow it up fairly quickly. This may be a chat during staff briefing or over a coffee at break time. It may entail a visit, armed with my diary to the new Head of History who expressed an interest in doing a project with his Year 10s. The NQT who wanted to reserve a book from the staff library will receive it in her pigeon-hole as soon as possible. The classroom support assistant who wanted ideas on brain gym will be told as soon as the book on order arrives. I feel it's important to respond to queries and requests straight away so that the LRC remains in the forefront of peoples' minds and so that they think of it as a helpful, efficient and effective service.

Conclusion

Staff induction is only the beginning of developing and maintaining good working relationships. At a time when schools are increasingly busy the LRC is just one cog in a complicated system. Staff induction is a bit like those taster tables you see in the supermarket, the ones with bite-size pieces of cheese or tiny cups of wine to sample and judge. I know that people will judge the LRC from what they see during the induction so I want to make absolutely sure the sample is enjoyable, memorable and will encourage them to come back for more.

Appendix 1a

National Literacy Strategy

Research and Study Skills Objectives Y5–7

How well do you know your objectives?

Please put a year by each of these

Objective	Year
Identify, sift and summarise the most important points or key ideas from a talk or discussion	
Make notes when listening for a sustained period and discuss how note-taking varies depending on context and purpose	
Extract the main points and relevant information from a text or source using a range of strategies such as skimming and scanning	
Select from a wide range of ICT programs to present text effectively and communicate information and ideas	
Make notes on and use evidence from across a text to explain events and ideas	
Make relevant notes when gathering ideas from texts	
Develop different ways of generating, organising and shaping ideas, using a range of planning formats or methods	
Appraise a text quickly deciding on its value, quality and usefulness	
Organise ideas into a coherent sequence of paragraphs	
Select information for a task from a range of sources and be aware of the relative strengths and weaknesses of these sources	
Make improvements to a piece of writing as it progresses by developing techniques for editing, proofreading and making revisions	
Locate resources for a specific task, appraising the value and relevance of information and acknowledging resources	
Reflect on reading habits and preferences and plan personal reading goals	
Identify the ways writers of non-fiction match language and organisation to their intentions	
Compare different types of narrative and information texts and identify how they are structured	
Acknowledge sources and recognise copyright	

Appendix 1b

National Literacy Strategy

Research and Study Skills Objectives Y5–7

How well do you know your objectives?

Please put a year by each of these

Objective	Year
Identify, sift and summarise the most important points or key ideas from a talk or discussion	Y7 Speaking and Listening
Make notes when listening for a sustained period and discuss how note-taking varies depending on context and purpose	Y6 Listening and Responding
Extract the main points and relevant information from a text or source using a range of strategies such as skimming and scanning	Y7 Reading for meaning
Select from a wide range of ICT programs to present text effectively and communicate information and ideas	Y6 Presentation
Make notes on and use evidence from across a text to explain events and ideas.	Y5 Understanding and Interpreting texts
Make relevant notes when gathering ideas from texts	Y7 Reading for meaning
Develop different ways of generating, organising and shaping ideas, using a range of planning formats or methods	Y7 Writing, Composition
Appraise a text quickly deciding on its value, quality and usefulness	Y6 Understanding and Interpreting Texts
Organise ideas into a coherent sequence of paragraphs	Y6/7 Text Structure and Organisation
Select information for a task from a range of sources and be aware of the relative strengths and weaknesses of these sources	Y7 (ICT – not a literacy objective
Make improvements to a piece of writing as it progresses by developing techniques for editing, proofreading and making revisions	Y7 Writing, Developing and using editing and proofreading skills
Locate resources for a specific task, appraising the value and relevance of information and acknowledging resources.	Y6/7 Understanding and Interpreting Texts
Reflect on reading habits and preferences and plan personal reading goals	Y5 Engaging with and Responding to Texts
Identify the ways writers of non-fiction match language and organisation to their intentions	Y6/7 Understanding and Interpreting Texts
Compare different types of narrative and information texts and identify how they are structured.	Y5 Understanding and Interpreting texts
Acknowledge sources and recognise copyright	Y7 (an ICT objective)

Appendix 2a

Making Links

with your usual partner primary/middle schools

☺ I could try this　　😐 I do this already　　☹ not suitable for me at present

Possible activity	☺	😐	☹
Ask your students or library helpers to create a library information booklet/poster/leaflet and upload or send copies to the partner schools for reference or with an attached competition/quiz			
Organise a link/blog to email questions and answers about the LRC and its use			
Invite the younger children and their teacher to visit you for some of their topic work or just for a 'field trip'			
Visit some of the schools yourself or with your library helpers to find out about their library, library experiences, reading habits and interests and work with transition units and to tell them about your LRC and what it has to offer			
Create a short presentation/PowerPoint about your library for use in the partner schools			
Create some web pages – perhaps including a virtual tour about the library for use in the partner schools			
Organise Y6/Y7 letter writing with a library and/or book theme			
Write a story/book – online? – with alternate chapters/sections by each school… or the writing and the illustrations			
Feature in the Summer Term Induction Day programme			
Feature in the information brochures sent to new parents			
Organise a joint Y6/Y7 book quiz or other book event			
Other ideas?			

Appendix 2b

Check List
for visiting a partner primary school

Please ✓ or ✗ as appropriate

Consult your line manager	
Consult the head of Y7/primary liaison team	
Visit after SATs and before the Induction Day, or in the Spring Term	
Produce clear aims for the visit	
Explain these aims to the primary school staff – how will they benefit?	
Take some of your library helpers with you to answer questions – especially if they are former pupils of the primary school	
Find out about their library and its use and find out about their book corner/reading habits etc., get them to give you a tour of the school and library and then talk about your LRC and perhaps read a story or two	
Answer questions (perhaps pulled from a hat!)	
Use some visual images – web pages, photos etc.	
Learn a name or two	
Could the children perhaps fill in a 'pupil profile' at this visit? or get them to write down five interesting facts about themselves for you to take away	
Take some of your in-house LRC book marks with your LRC info. on them	
Get them to write a few lines on 'what I'd like to find in my big school LRC'	
Wear your big badge so they remember who you are!	
Get them to email you some answers to some questions you left behind	
Take them some 'fascinating facts' about your LRC – some true some false and get them thinking about them or checking your web pages etc to see which ones are true!	
Take some exciting resources with you to show them	
Find out about their Literacy work and work with the Transition units as well as their library experiences – local as well as school library	

LRC Profile

Appendix 3

Please tell us about yourself

Name and Tutor Group:	I read in these
Languages:	
My primary school was:	

Please circle either Yes or No

My previous school had a library	Yes / No	Story books were kept in the library	Yes / No
Story books were kept in our classroom	Yes / No	Non-fiction books were kept in the library	Yes / No
Information books were kept in number/Dewey order	Yes / No	I used to borrow books from the school library	Yes / No
I was a library helper in my primary school	Yes / No	I belong to the public library	Yes / No
I enjoy reading	Yes / No	I often use the public library	Yes / No

Please tell us

The sorts of books I like are about
The book I am reading at present is
My favourite time for reading is
My favourite place for reading is
My favourite magazine is

Do you ... use a computer at home? Yes No
use Internet for information finding? Yes No
use chatrooms? Yes No
use email? Yes No

Tell us about a project that you did at school in Year 5 or Year 6 that involved using the library and what you enjoyed about it.

Appendix 4

Top 20
Induction Activities
to welcome, motivate and inspire

1	complete a 'library locator' map	
2	obtain information about/discuss the library's 'code of conduct'	
3	move round answering a quiz/worksheet about different features etc. or do a jigsaw created out of a digi photo of the LRC or identify odd photos of resources and parts of the LRC	
4	learn how to borrow a book, browse and actually borrow one of their choice	
5	browse the ICT	
6	carry out an alphabetical order/fiction activity – perhaps finding specific books by a named author e.g. Michael Morpurgo/Jacqueline Wilson	
7	carry out a Dewey activity – 'code buster' or locate specific non-fiction books	
8	create questions for a general question/answer session	
9	listen to a story (or story extract), read perhaps by you	
10	carry out a card sequence activity using the school's/library's Steps to Learning sequence	
11	watch/discuss a video about the library	
12	browse the LRC webpages or LRC multimedia authoring package	
13	design a library of the future poster	
14	answer a questionnaire about their library experiences or choose the book they would most like to have written (for a display maybe)	
15	try out the LRC's catalogue/issue system	
16	look at a range of resources on a specific topic they will be looking at in one curriculum area – perhaps History, English or Science – maybe as a Treasure Hunt	
17	create a poster about interesting information they discover	
18	receive a library certificate/book mark for successful task completion	
19	hear you introduce yourself, your work and your potential to give help/advice	
20	discuss their previous school library experiences – how/why/when did they use it? or what they hope for their new LRC experiences	

Appendix 5

Induction Certificate

The following student

_____

from tutor group _____

has successfully followed and completed the

Student Induction Training Programme

This student has

- ☐ borrowed and returned a book
- ☐ found a fiction book by a named author
- ☐ found an information book on a particular subject
- ☐ browsed three websites on a topic
- ☐ answered questions on the 'code of conduct'
- ☐ filled in the 'Please Tell Us About You' profile
- ☐ browsed the library web pages
- ☐ created a poster with 'fascinating facts' on it
- ☐ taken part in a question and answer session
- ☐ watched the LRC video
- ☐ learned about the school's Steps to Learning sequence

Well Done!

Signed: _____ (Librarian)   Date: _____

Signed: _____ (Tutor)   Date: _____

Sixth Form LRC Contract

LRC staff are delighted to welcome you as a Sixth Form user of our range of LRC services.

We will try at all times to support your study by:

- Providing a positive environment for study
- By answering your enquiries effectively
- By providing a range of resources suitable for your courses and interests
- By providing links to outside information services
- By consulting you as we make changes to make our services more effective for you

In return we ask that you agree to the following:

- To use the LRC as a place of quiet study
- To accept the school's LRC code of conduct
- To accept the school's Acceptable Use of ICT procedures

If you have any concerns about LRC use we hope you will discuss them with us. Thank you.

Signed: (Pupil)   Date: Tutor Group:

Signed: (Librarian)   Date:

Appendix 7

LRC Induction
for adults new to the school
Who needs what?

Group	Information
Head Teacher or other member of SMT	
Teaching staff	
Teaching Assistants / Learning Support Workers	
Admin staff	
Governors	
PTA members	
Parents	

Supplement: Short Story

The Adventures of Wordsworth the Library Owl

'Perfect Peace and Quiet'

Written by Marie Hewitt

Illustrated by Anne Taylor

Story Supplement

It was Friday evening, the end of a long week in the school library, and what a week it had been! The children had all gone home for the weekend, the librarian had heaved a huge sigh of relief when the bell rang at half past three and she'd gone home too. She'd 'blown her top' that afternoon because one particular class – (……) I think it was – had left the library in a terrible mess, books all over the place and the chairs not put away properly. The cleaners and the caretaker had left as well, and the library had been locked and it was almost dark.

Perfect peace and quiet, you might think – not a bit of it – well, not on this particular Friday anyway! It had been such a dreadful week that none of the books could settle down and relax for the weekend.

There was such a commotion going on in the reference section, where a three-cornered argument was in progress between the encyclopedia, the dictionary and the atlas. There was almost as much noise coming from the fiction section, where the paperbacks were having a right old moan about one thing and another. On top of that, coughing, sneezing, groaning, and even the sound of someone crying could be heard!

Coughing, sneezing, groaning, and even the sound of someone crying could be heard

Story Supplement

A three-cornered argument was in progress between the encyclopedia, the dictionary and the atlas

Suddenly, from a space on the wall, a large bird fluttered down, and with an enormous screech, landed on the librarian's desk. It was Wordsworth of course, the library owl. He had been so disturbed by all the noise that he had flown down to investigate.

Now, you might wonder how an owl ever came to be in the library in the first place. Well, when Wordsworth was quite small, he had been rather naughty and had flown away from his nest. Being a very inquisitive little owl, he had decided to investigate an open window in the school library, and had somehow managed to get himself locked in for the night. He had been so distressed and frightened that night, but the books felt sorry for him and had been so kind to him that they became friends and asked him to stay. The pupils in the school were so excited when they found him in the library next morning that they adopted him as the library mascot and called him Wordsworth.

Now Wordsworth had been listening very intently to the arguing and grumbling that was going on that night. 'What on earth is the matter with you all?' he demanded. 'For goodness sake, it's Friday. We've got two whole days of peace and quiet, no disturbances or interruptions, no noisy kids rummaging through our shelves, two whole days in which to relax and recharge our batteries ready for Monday morning, and in any case, you know I can't allow all this noise. The library is a "quiet" room. The librarian would have a fit if she could hear you all now.'

Story Supplement

But Wordsworth was a very wise owl – well, owls always are, aren't they, or so everyone tells us, and although he was cross with the books for being so noisy, he was wise enough to realise that there must be a jolly good reason why the books were behaving so badly.

'Who is going to tell me what all this is about?' asked Wordsworth. Of course all the books started to shout and talk at the same time.

'No, no', screeched Wordsworth, 'this isn't getting us anywhere! I suggest we have a proper meeting, and each section of the books in the library – the fiction, the non-fiction and the reference section – can each have a representative to speak on their behalf, and if we're going to do this properly, we need someone to take notes.'

*'Me, me, oh please let it be me,' begged the **Guinness Book of Records**. 'I'd love to do it, and I'm the obvious one for the job, after all, I'm brilliant at keeping records.' Wordsworth agreed, and after adjusting his spectacles on the end of his beak, which made him look very intelligent and rather distinguished, he declared that the meeting should commence. 'We'll hear from the reference section first,' he decided. 'After all, they were making the most noise! Now just what was it that you were all arguing about?'*

An encyclopedia straightened himself confidently on the shelf and began. 'We were arguing about which one of us is the most important book in the library. A bit pointless really, there's no question about it, is there? It's quite obvious, it's me! I know everything there is to know about everything!'

'Me, me, oh please let it be me,' begged the Guinness Book of Records

Story Supplement

'I think that's quite enough,' interrupted Wordsworth, who was getting very exasperated by this stupid bickering.

'Is that so Mr Know-all?' retorted the dictionary on the shelf below. The encyclopedia was such a bighead that all the other books in the library called him Mr Know-all. A little unkind you might think. Well, the encyclopedia was so vain and conceited that he was actually flattered and took it as a compliment! 'I totally disagree with you,' continued Dickie the dictionary. 'I must be more important than you. I can tell you about nearly every word in the English language, and show you how to spell it and pronounce it.'

'Oh no you can't,' snapped Globetrotter the atlas, affectionately known as Trotter to his friends. 'Well, not every word anyway. I have the names of every town, city and country in my index. You don't have those words, do you?'

'Well, maybe not,' replied Dickie, for once lost for words. 'Anyway, my name is Richard, not Dickie, so please be so kind as to remember that I am a dictionary and that I don't take kindly to abbreviations.'

'I think that's quite enough,' interrupted Wordsworth, who was getting very exasperated by this stupid bickering. 'You are all being very silly. I'm really surprised at books in your position behaving so childishly. You are all equally important, so important in fact that you need to be here all the time for the children to use you whenever they need to.'

'And that's another thing, while we're on the subject,' piped up Globetrotter the atlas. 'In my line of business I would like to travel, but oh no, we're not

Story Supplement

even allowed out! We don't get to go on any adventures, never get to see what's inside some of those rather interesting schoolbags, or get to ride in cars or on buses. We're just stuck here on the same old shelves, same old views, day after day. BORING!'

'He's right, you know,' added Dickie (sorry, Richard) the dictionary. 'All the other non-fiction books are allowed out. Some of them are even chosen to go on display and show off their front covers, downright favouritism if you ask me, and the fiction books, well, they're always off out, several times a week some of them. You can never find them in, it's just not fair! In any case, I can't understand why they're so popular. Stories, that's all they are, a load of make-believe, not about real things like the rest of us!'

'Excuse me, excuse me,' a nervous little voice ventured from the paperback rack. 'Excuse me, but you might not enjoy being one of us for very long, the way we get treated sometimes. Not everyone looks after us properly you know. We're not as strong as you chaps, with our bendy covers, and a lot of us have bad backs as well. We often return from our outings feeling very under the weather, and some of us never get brought back at all. Two weeks is the limit you know! Anyway, you non-fiction books don't know how lucky you are having your pictures taken on that machine over there, and you've all got fancy numbers stuck on your spines. We fiction books haven't you know.'

'That's because we're far more organised than you,' argued a rather boring looking book in the science section.

'Of course we're organised,' snapped the fiction paperback. 'Our authors, the people who wrote us, know how to organise us. We don't need numbers, we've got names!'

'Oh do stop this nonsense,' sighed Wordsworth. 'You're giving me a headache. Perhaps the fiction paperback would like to explain why they all feel so unhappy.'

'Well,' began the fiction paperback, 'it's like this … Most of the pupils treat us very well. They wash their hands before handling us, and put us in plastic bags to keep us clean and dry. See those two over there?' she added, pointing to two rather soggy looking books draped untidily over the radiator. 'They came back today soaking wet and looking very flushed – lovely shade of pink! Blackcurrant juice, so we heard, spilled inside someone's bag. They're already coughing and sneezing, probably end up with pneumonia I shouldn't wonder! Two of our colleagues have had to take early retirement because they were unfit for duty. A Roald Dahl book was really choked, had his pages stuck together with chewing gum. YUK! And another, well, he hurled himself into the waste bin in despair. Well, how would you feel if you were all greasy and smelled of salt and vinegar? Would anyone ever want to take you out again?'

Story Supplement

'A Roald Dahl book was really choked, had his pages stuck together with chewing gum. YUK!'

Just then, the paperback was interrupted by the sound of groaning coming from the windowsill. Wordsworth flew over and landed next to a very sad-looking little book. 'What's the matter with you little chap?' he enquired.

'I feel so awful. I've got a bad back you know. One of the children bent me almost double and I feel as if I'm falling apart!'

'What you need is a bit of support,' Wordsworth decided, and he gently picked up the injured book in his beak and popped him between two sturdy hardbacks, who snuggled up to him on either side and soon had him feeling much stronger.

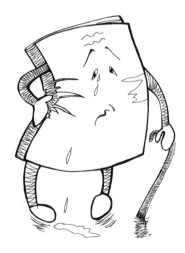

'I've got a bad back you know. One of the children bent me almost double and I feel as if I'm falling apart!'

Story Supplement

'I'm lost forever,' sobbed Kicker the football book.
'Who's going to think of looking for me here?'

No sooner was this problem sorted out than Wordsworth thought he could hear someone crying over there in the animal section. He flew over and there, sure enough, among the animal books, was Kicker, the football book.

'What on earth are you doing here, Kicker?' asked Wordsworth. 'You're way out of place.'

'I know,' sobbed the football book. 'I'm lost forever, no one will ever be able to find me now, even though I've got my proper number on my spine. Who's going to think of looking for me here?'

'Now dry up those tears, a big fit chap like you, we'll soon have you back in your proper place.' And no sooner said than it was done.

By now the books had begun to settle down. They all felt a lot better because they had been able to tell someone about their problems. Wordsworth was troubled, however. He was worried that some of the books were still unhappy.

'Something will have to be done about it! I must speak to the librarian on Monday morning,' he declared. 'But I tell you what', he suggested to the books. 'Why don't you all relax now and I'll ask one of the fiction books to tell you a story.'